B

Language

Learn How to Use Dark Psychology, Mind Control
and Nlp Techniques to Influence Anyone

(Read Facial Expressions Using Mind Hacking)

Marshall S. Sorense

Published by Kevin Dennis

Marshall S. Sorense

Body Language: Learn How to Use Dark Psychology, Mind Control and Nlp Techniques to Influence Anyone (Read Facial Expressions Using Mind Hacking)

ISBN 978-1-989920-17-6

Legal & Disclaimer

The information contained in this book is not designed to replace or take the place of any form of medicine or professional medical advice. The information in this book has been provided for educational and entertainment purposes only.

The information contained in this book has been compiled from sources deemed reliable, and it is accurate to the best of the Author's knowledge; however, the Author cannot guarantee its accuracy and validity and cannot be held liable for any errors or omissions. Changes are periodically made to this book. You must consult your doctor or get professional medical advice before using any of the suggested remedies, techniques, or information in this book.

Table of Contents

Introduction

A lot of men have a hard time in the dating world. This isn't because they don't have redeeming qualities, but because talking to women can be hard without the right information. The following chapters will discuss some of the many methods and techniques for building attraction with women and getting them to open up to you, paving the way for positive dating experiences. This relies a lot on accurately reading her emotions and thoughts and responding to them, along with having the right mindset about yourself. Contrary to popular belief, talking to women isn't hard and this book will show you how true that is.

You will discover how important it is to come across as confident, show that you're listening to her, and feel okay with yourself during conversations with women. Oftentimes, expectations cause reality, and this can be used to your advantage. You will learn which questions to ask, how to use your tone of voice for increasing chemistry, and the reasons behind the importance of reading her nonverbal cues. The final chapter will explore specific body language cues you can look for and decipher to figure out how you're doing with a woman you're attempting to get to know.

There are plenty of books on this subject on the market, thanks again for choosing this one! Every effort was made to ensure it is full of as much useful information as possible. Please enjoy!

Congratulations on downloading your personal copy of the Talking to Women: How to Build Attraction through Communication. Thank you for doing so.

Chapter 1: Read People Instantly

The Power Of Persuasion

Do you want to read people's mind? Do you want to know how to understand people instantly? Many scientists and experts say that it is impossible to read the mind of people and follow them by just looking at them. They are right, and you will never know that person unless you talked to him a lot, go with him often and hung out with him.

In marketing and sales, it is essential that you can read people instantly because you are not going to meet just one person per day. You will never go anywhere by that.

There is one powerful tool that will help you read people instantly and instantly you can get what you want. The tool is not a thing, it is in you, and you just need to develop it. It is the power and art of persuasion that is hidden in you.

Every one of us has its hidden persuasion. You just need to exercise and train yourselves on how to use them primarily reading people.

Reading people instantly is not that easy, but with the power of persuasion, you will learn how to read people immediately. You will learn that persuasive technique in here.

The power of persuasion can help you pull out something from the affluent, and that's how you are going to read and understand them.

There are different ways on how you can read people but only this art of persuasion that you can read them instantly. Like for example, you can read people through their body language. You will know if that person is interested in you by his body language.

Another example that you can read people but only these powers of persuasion you can pull them out instantly are the facial expressions and eye movement. Just even the facial expression, you can read a lot from that.

Your persuasion technique will help you determine what's with that expression, did they understand you, and do they believe in you or trust you? Your persuasion and how you persuade people will answer that question instantly.

Emotional Intelligence

People think no one knows them like the way they do. People maintain that they are more familiar with their houses than anybody else is.

They assert that they have far more knowledge about their neighbourhood when compared with others. People just like to profess that they understand their lives inside out. On the other hand, about emotions and personalities, the truth is quite contrary to what is stated.

We are inclined to turn a blind eye about our failings. We would like to believe that we are aware of our emotions and personalities well, but the fact is that a majority of people overlook their shortcomings.

For instance, let us take emotional intelligence. When a person gets to know about the significance of EI, without much ado, he starts to dwell on people whom he feels are bereft of emotional intelligence. Not many people take the trouble to look at themselves to find out if they are devoid of EI.

It is for this reason that a person requires undergoing intelligence tests. Now, a person should understand just to what extent the matter of emotional intelligence tends to shape his life.

The best possible way to make someone realize his limitations is to cause them to become conscious of it. Now, if somebody came near you just now and stated that you were without EI, is it possible for you to accept it as real?

A person has to be presented evidence regarding his failings before he is convinced.

The advantage of tests on emotional intelligence lies in the fact that these tests give you an opportunity to confirm directly how right you were about the observation of yourself.

By going through a test on emotional intelligence, you may expose yourself to the likelihood that you do not just know yourself the way you believe you do.

This alteration in assessment makes it easier for you to modify your way of thinking with the intention that you become more aware of the need to change for the better.

A further benefit of undertaking a test on emotional intelligence is that it makes it possible for a person to identify precisely that particular portion of emotional intelligence that he is found wanting. Using a test of emotional knowledge, it is possible for a person to gather as to which section of emotional intelligence needs his attention.

Emotional intelligence tests, besides, make it easy for someone to appreciate the prospect of possessing emotional intelligence. By way of these EI tests, a person discovers how to avail himself of emotional intelligence, each day of his life. Due to this, a person can lead a far more contented and successful life.

Moreover, emotional intelligence tests too can enlighten a person just to what extent he can connect with other people.

Now, the social interface can prove to be enormously significant in one's life. This is dead right. You could be either an employee or a student, but you require others to lend a hand as you travel down life's way.

Tests on emotional intelligence can assist you to improve your aptitude to sense the way other people feel. This attitude enables you to identify with those around you. Insight is the basis of knowledge. When you are capable of securing some awareness about a person's emotions, then you should not have any difficulty in counting him as part of your inner circle.

Tests on emotional intelligence are lovely since they permit a person to observe the facts. It is common knowledge that the top barrier to truth is found in one's self. A test on emotional intelligence can negotiate a person's resistance and permit that person to assess himself without prejudice.

NLP Eye Accessing Cues

NLP eye accessing cues give the adage "eyes are the windows to the soul" a whole new meaning. This means that the direction in which our eyes move reveals whether we're remembering something or imagining something new.

By learning about these different cues, you can drastically improve your current persuasion skills. You should try and read this to find out how NLP eye accessing cues can help you in understanding people's minds and persuading people to do what you want.

To start with, you must first learn which eye cues correspond to the different senses.

If a person is trying to remember or recall an image, their eyes will probably move up to their left. If a person is trying to imagine or "visually construct" a new image, their eyes will step up to their right.

If a person is trying to remember a sound, their eyes will most likely turn to their immediate left. If a person is trying to imagine how a group of musical notes, for example, would sound like, their eyes will move to their immediate right.

Other parts of our senses, as well as your emotions, also have different NLP eye accessing cues. If a person is dealing with smell, tastes, touch and emotions, their eyes will probably move to their downward right. And if a person is talking to himself or herself mentally (or otherwise), the eyes will most likely move downward left.

Application Of NLP Eye Accessing Cues

Equipping yourself with this information helps you spot whether a person is lying through their teeth or entertaining a new idea. So let's say you ask someone,

"Where were you when the child fell?" If they look up to the right, they might be making up a story to cover the real incident. If they look up to the left, they might be recalling what happened (in reality).

This method may help you determine if you want to accept their explanation or not, while also taking into account other factors.

You can also take advantage of this information to appear more honest or trustworthy. For example, if you want your story to seem more believable, make sure to follow the right NLP eye accessing cues to come across as genuine.

Knowing these cues by heart can also come quite handy in selling. If your target, for example, finds himself or herself having an internal dialogue about buying a brand new car, then you'll know that one way to persuade them is to present to them the pros and cons of making the bold purchase yourself (focusing more on the advantages, of course) and cutting off the

customer's opportunity to convince
himself or herself otherwise.

Chapter 2: How Internal Communication

Influences

Body Language

"We here today all know that communication is essential for the economic, social and political betterment of mankind." Mr. Gerald Cross, Secretary General of International Telecommunication Union in delivering a speech during 1965 Amateur Radio and International Union conference in San Jose, California, July 4 pointed this out.

You can add the psychological and the spiritual to the mix in order to bring effective human communication full circle. Five decades of scientific and technological improvements have passed since those distant days. Breakthroughs in communication, and human body language continues to confuse experts in every industry. How much body language do you use to communicate at work, in social gatherings, business and at home?

You would not know precisely how much unless you understand the importance of connectivity and connection in the lives of humans.

Connectivity and Connection

You have read of the law of attraction. You've heard of telepathy – "communication taking place between two different people in thought form." None of these forms of sharing thoughts and ideas would be possible if you were not physical, psychological and spiritual in nature. What is the connection between these three aspects of human life?

Connectivity of thought happens in the invisible world. This is where thoughts, feelings and emotions are formed. The outward demonstration is manifested in the physical world through the body. This phenomenon happens when random strangers connect through intimate communication, sometimes in an airport, train station, or diner in the middle of the night.

All actions in the physical world are governed by natural laws. Scientists have been relying for centuries on the Laws of Thermodynamics or Newton's Law of Motion. Refresh your memory on the distinction between the three human aspects: the physical, psychological and the spiritual discussed earlier in chapter two of this study.

Creation Theories

Connectivity and interconnectivity between plants, animals and human beings trace origin back to the original source – Supernatural Being many refer to as GOD. This applies if you believe in the creation theory of the universe. However, if you think evolution and chance theories hold true, you may want to spend some serious time rethinking why you believe such things.

You don't need scientific proof to believe there is harmony on the universe. Simply watch plant and human life. Intelligent design proposes that life, or the universe, cannot have risen by chance. Its designs are super complicated, leading to the belief that it was designed. The universe, and all aspects of life within it, were created by an intelligent entity. Based on the theory that an intelligent design could not have been brought into being by chance events, how will you plan to think more purposefully about the world around you? Try detaching yourself from the physical and tune into the psychological or - spiritual. You may need to lay aside the life-long assumptions that you've read in books and heard from lectures. Your eye of understanding will capture and present pictures of a perfect universe. A universe that lies beyond the horizon. Give your mind the opportunity to explore the organized universe and the force behind its existence.

Eye of Understanding

You discover the sky isn't a limit but simply the distance to which your physical eyes can stretch. Your spiritual "eye of understanding," is capable of penetrating the deep blue sky to bring to mind both the living sounds and sights of a world beyond. It can connect your physical and psychological experiences, in the spiritual world, to the galaxy. Occasionally people return to life after being pronounced dead with tales of a celestial world beyond the realm of human imagination. Even the Apostle Paul, in 2 Corithians 12:4, explained how he was caught up into paradise, and experienced things that even he was not permitted to speak about.

Science has made great discoveries and opened a window into the unknown. Yet scientific discoveries pale in comparison to God's ingenuity of bringing into existence life and matching souls to human bodies.

Have you read of the scientific breakthrough of making sperms and female eggs? You haven't? That is because it has never been accomplished. Sperm banks would be of no value if science could create life. Human beings can't rely on scientific research to manufacture sperms. It hardly seems worth and time and energy to research such a project when the original processes work so well. Why reinvent the wheel?

Science and Technology

Of course the technology to preserve and fertilize eggs which are planted into a woman's womb is available. These advances can aid in bringing about a pregnancy where infertility problems exist, but creating life from scratch is beyond human capability. Sperms and female eggs are manufactured by body, but the organized program needed to continue life on Planet Earth through procreation is bigger than mankind.

Human life still baffles scientists because only God knows the recipe. He alone holds the patent of life and jealously guards it. No one has access to that patent, and that is the reason God alone matches bodies to souls.

No matter what theory of origins you choose, creation, or evolution and chance, you cannot contradict the facts concerning the of connectivity between living things.

18

If you need proof, take a careful look around you at nature. You can't deny there is a connection between you and the animals, plants, sea life and birds of the air. You can accept this connection without understanding all the details. A simple study of the food chain and the water cycle will remind you how closely linked you are to the world you live in.

Plants, animals and human beings share a common ancestry with all living things, birds of the air, fish and insects. Yet in the ways that you're special and unique; so your body language communication is unique.

"An individual remains an individual not only from birth to death but actually long, before birth, until long after death," Joel Goldsmith, author of Infinite Way observed.

How Individual Uniqueness Influences Body Language Communication

Individual uniqueness may not be as pronounced and manifested in the spiritual realm, as it is in the physical world. But even though facts of proof concerning spiritual uniqueness is difficult to observe and record scientifically, the individual human in the physical world differs from one soul to the next.

"None can duplicate my brush strokes, none can make my chisel marks, none can duplicate my handwriting...." Og Mandino, an American author, wrote in The Legend of the Ten Scrolls. Nothing is better than knowing you're a masterpiece of creation.

The lyrics to the following song were written by Wayne Watson and beautifully portrays the value of anything when touched by a master.

"Touch Of The Master's Hand"
Well it was battered and scared, And the auctioneer felt it was hardly worth his while, To waste much time on the old violin but he held it up with a smile, Well it sure ain't much but its all we got left I guess we aught to sell it to, Oh, now who'll start the bid on this old violin? Just one more and we'll be through.

And then he cried one give me one dollar, Who'll make it two only two dollars who'll make it three, Three dollars twice now that's a good price, Now who's gonna bid for me? Raise up your hand now don't wait any longer the auctions about to end, Who's got four Just one dollar more to bid on this old violin?

Well the air was hot and the people stood around as the sun was setting low, From the back of the crowd a gray haired man, Came forward and picked up the bow, He wiped the dust from the old violin then he tightened up the strings, Then he played out a melody pure and sweet, sweeter than the Angels sing, And then the music stopped and the auctioneer, With a voice that was quiet and low he said now what am I bid, For this old violin and he held it up with a bow.

And then he cried out one give me one thousand, Who'll make it two only two thousand who'll make it three, Three thousand twice you know that's a good price, Common who's gonna to bid for me? And the people cried out what made the change we don't understand, Then the auctioneer stopped and he said with a smile, It was the touch of the Master's hand.

You know there's many a man with his life out of tune, Battered and scared with sin and he's auctioned cheap, To a thankless world much like that old violin, Oh, but then the Master comes, And that old foolish crowd they never understand, The worth of a soul and the change that is rought, Just by one touch of the Masters hand.

And then he cried out one give me one thousand, Who'll make it two only two thousand who'll make it three, Three thousand twice you know that's a good price, Common who's gonna bid for me? And the people cried out what made the change we don't understand, Then the auctioneer stopped and he said with a smile, It was the touch, that's all it was; it was the touch of the Master's hand, It was the touch of the Master's hand; oh, it was the touch of the Master's hand.

"In a broken nest there are no whole eggs," a Chinese proverb says. This quote portrays a picture of disharmony on the universe by expressing the truth that a fractured environment cannot support a healthy soul. However, the existence of the invisible strand of power which holds and maintains all things in perfect harmony is undeniable. One scripture proclaims, "By Him all things consist, are held together." This strand can be detected even throughout the seven characteristics which make body- language communication possible.

Seven Characteristics of Body Language Communication

1. Impulsive

Communication is dynamic. It's an on-going process. It moves back and forth from sender to receiver in the form of feedback and interaction. You'll read about feedback later in chapter six. Human beings change and grow as individuals and so does communication patterns and the interpretation of body-language communication. The changes are also noticeable from one place to another.

2. Interactive

Communication occurs between people. It also occurs internally. The internal communication, explained in chapter two, always involves the three aspects of human life: physical, psychological and the spiritual. Refer back to this chapter to become better acquainted with conscious, and sub conscious communication, and the intellect necessary in body- language communication. Even during a conversation with a friend, you may find yourself having an internal chat with your mind and attitude. Do you agree with your friend's viewpoint? Are you responding emotionally to the various points he is trying to make? Do you argue with your friend internally?

3. Indefinite

Communication produces negative or positive results. The basis behind various reactions changes from one person to the next or one scenario and another. Outside of context, responses to body-language communication cannot always be predicted. The simple question, "What are you doing?" can have a variety of responses based upon the circumstances of the situation and the relationship or tone of the questioner. An angry mother who finds her three-year old drawing on the walls with permanent ink would ask that question with a different tone, than the new boyfriend trying to strike up a conversation with his girlfriend on the phone. Communication, therefore, can take various conversation tracks depending on the circumstances surrounding it.

4. Irreversible

A Chinese proverb says, "A word rashly spoken cannot be brought back even by a chariot or four horses." In the heat of the moment you may use violent, unproductive communication only to regret having used those harsh words. One mentor illustrated the harm that gossip can produce in the fragile community of family and friends. He took the offending gossiper to the top of the town's tallest building. When the repentant young man regretted speaking lies about a colleague and wished to undo the damage, the patient teacher gently pulled out his method of driving home a point. The teacher glanced sadly at the young student and handed him a feather pillow. "Cut open the pillow and shake out all the feathers over the side of the building," the master advised. "Now," the wise man said once all the feathers were floating down from the roof top, "go down and find every feather and place it back into the pillow case." When the young man objected to the proposal, claiming that it would be impossible to retrieve each feather, the teacher wisely drove home his point. "Angry, harmful words-like these feathers- can easily leave your mouth, but is impossible to reverse entirely the damage done. Even an apology cannot fully erase the pain from the memory of the one who you spoke to so harshly." Grieved, the young gossiper vowed to always be more careful of letting angry words fly out of his mouth.

Unwisely spoken words portray a lack of control. A proverb says, "He that has no control over his own spirit is like a city that is broken down and without walls." In the case of internal communication, speaking harmful, negative words to yourself leads to disillusionment. Your own view of yourself can be altered by negative self-talk. Interpersonal communication it is the outward demonstration of your conversation. Speaking kindly to yourself can help you to learn of to speak kindly to others.

Another proverb says, "Speaking without thinking is like shooting without aiming." And if you do cause wounds by harsh speaking, the Bible says, "A soft answer turns a way wrath."

5. Involvement

Communication between the conscious and the sub conscious aspects of our personalities work in harmony to produce desired results in life. Jesus once said, "As a man thinks in his own heart, so is he." You become the person that you develop through internal conversation. The two, pulling in separate opposite directions, only create conflict, retard growth and slow down life. You can look in the mirror and physically say to yourself that you are awesome, but if your spirit counters that with a negative response, you could find yourself slipping backwards in personal growth.

6. Increases Commitment

The more you engage the mind on positive thinking, the more that positive can thoughts take center stage in your mind. This permits you more chances for you to create and exhibit positive body language.

7. Contextual

Communication has no meaning apart from its surrounding. The simple command "move" can take on significance depending on the situation. In a simple setting, a mother can place a hand on a child's shoulder to move him aside to be able to reach something on the top shelf. I a different circumstance, the word "move" can become a warning to get a person out of the path of a falling boulder.

All of these aspects can be simply concluded by saying that communication does not take place in a vacuum.

Section One Summary

Chapter one explains the distinction between verbal and nonverbal communication based on facts from research. This chapter also gives a sneak peak of chapter six by pointing out that effective communication goes beyond Verbal and Nonverbal to include three aspects of human life, physical, psychological and spiritual. These three aspects of human life definitely influence internal communication which cuts across the seven signal systems to be discussed in chapter seven.

How Body Language Fits In the Ideal Pattern Of Communication

All body movements convey meaning. However, meanings vary from place to place, culture to culture, country to country and continent to continent. There are three distinct notable classifications of body language commonly used in most cases. This section of the book explores the three distinct classifications of body language communication.

1. Physical – Scratching, winking, stretching, yawning all some of most common outward body movements.
2. Psychological – Intellect.
3. Social – Touching

Read about scratching, winking and stretching physical classification in chapter three. Engage your intellect with psychological insights on body language in chapter four and touch base with social body language communication in chapter five.

When verbal communication breaks down as it does many times in life, body language offers alternative escape route to create understanding between people. Whether you use the hand, arm, head, or trunk, all body part movements communicate messages. This is observed when a deaf person and a hearing person attempt to communicate.

You read how the three aspects of human life the physical, psychological land spiritual influence body language communication in chapter two. The subject of this book is on body language communication. Therefore, you can't have body language without a body.

You're a physical human being. You're also psychological and social being. These three aspects of human life influence body language communication.

In section one chapter one and two, you read of the connection between three aspects of human beings: the physical, psychological and the spiritual. The emphasis on body language communication in these chapters is on the individual. The next three chapters three through five digs deep into the three distinct body language communication classifications – physical, psychological and social. Let's get started on our exploration

in on this section on the physical aspects
of body language communication.

Chapter 3: Understanding The Human Mind

The human mind (brain) is the most powerful organ in the human body. Only the human mind can rationalize, solve problems and perform cognitive functions that no other living being can do. This is the major reason why you differ from animals – you have a rational, thinking brain.

It's also the mind that allows you to perform all the cognitive, physical and emotional ideas that you have planned. Without the brain acknowledging your goal to analyze people, nothing would happen; your body won't act the way you want it to. This is because the brain is the center of the nervous system. Every act passes through the brain, and the brain has to trigger it to happen.

Formation of basic beliefs and thoughts

There are multiple factors that influence the way you think and the way your thoughts are generated. These factors start from the day you were conceived in the womb of your mother. Yes, that's right – as soon as the sperm cell penetrates the ovum, your "indoctrination" begins.

Various scientific studies established the connection between the mother's behavior and practices and the condition of the fetus. Undoubtedly, alcohol consumption, intake of prohibited drugs and smoking have detrimental effects on the fetus. These substances can damage the organs of the fetus - including the brain. The worst effect is for the baby to become a "blue baby" – dead at birth.

It was also observed that mothers who viewed their pregnancy negatively had a child who has "poorer emotional regulation and attention."

The role of heredity and environment in a person's mental abilities

When a person is born, there are two main factors that affect the growth and development of the baby. These are his genes and the environment in which he would thrive in.

You inherit your genes from both your father and mother, and these genes will leave a mark primarily on your physical, physiological attributes and mental abilities. You inherit your blood type, the color of your skin, eyes and hair. Your intellect is a combination of the IQ of your parents.

Thus, the mental capacity of a person comes also from his genes. The environment will then either hone or stymie the development of the person's intellectual abilities.

This is the reason why when judging a person; you have to consider his background and environment.

The environment as a crucial factor in the formation of a person's beliefs

The environment in which the individual has grown affects his way of thinking. If a person grew in a family where violence is a common occurrence, he will end up thinking violence is acceptable and is a common practice.

Another example is when a person is showered with love throughout his growing up years. He would naturally think that love is a given.

When he goes out into the world, he would later learn that there are people devoid of love, and that not every person would love him. This will also develop him into a good or bad person, depending on the support and advices that he would receive.

This is how your mind evolves and develops. Some people may be exposed to traumatic experiences, which would scar them for life and affect the way they think.

Most probably the person's beliefs would be something like, "People are unkind, so I have to protect myself at all times."

Power of the mind

However, as human beings, you have the power to create your own life. As the popular cliché goes, "Life is 10% of what happens to you and 90% of how you react to it." It's all about attitude. You must train yourself to stay firm and do something you plan to do, and not just flow with the water, wherever it may lead you.

Despite the role of heredity and environment, you still have the power to direct your life towards success and happiness.

How? By changing the way you think.

You want to analyze people? Then commit yourself towards this goal as if your life depended on it.

Believe that you can do it, and you can. You are what you think you are. Psyche yourself - every morning and evening - that you believe you would be able to accomplish the task. Look at yourself in the mirror and say, "I can read people's minds. I can read people's minds...I will succeed...."

Do this every day and soon your subconscious will catch on. When the subconscious becomes aware of your goal, together with your conscious mind, they will act together to help you succeed.

Of course, as you psyche yourself, you have to practice the skill. It's a skill so you can only acquire it, when you practice it.

It's like riding a bike. You can only learn how to ride a bike, if you actually ride one and practice.

In addition, you have to be aware that your mind is powerful and could affect your body's responses to certain events. Without your brain commanding your body, your body won't be able to move a muscle or lift a finger. That's how powerful your mind is.

Also, you have learned how the mind works and the reasons behind the thoughts and beliefs of people. Use this as a tool in reading and analyzing people.

Chapter 4: Benefits Of Analyzing People

For self-development, it's really important to study human behavior. You can learn a lot by observing and adapting the actions or conducts of other people, and analyze the reason behind those actions and behavior. Human psychology came into existence as a behavioral neuroscience feature.

There are many great benefits of analyzing people. It helps you with good business deals, better relations, better opportunities, and it has a greater impact on the society we live in the present day. As the thoughts shape-up, people, in turn, shape the social order. Therefore, studying and improving these thought patterns can help to develop a better individual and a safer society. It can also help to encourage acceptance, compassion, independent reasoning and thinking among people within the structure of the society. Beliefs or morals may differ considerably from person to person but behavioral science won't.

Analyzing people also helps you to comprehend and value people more. It helps you to know what drives or triggers-off people. They do not mean to hurt others all the time; it's just the way they are. This ability helps you consider people in more optimistic ways. It allows you to comprehend the actual motives behind certain actions, reactions or responses of the people in a better way.

Following are some of the great benefits of analyzing people:

1.) Being Understanding and Compassionate

Due to your people analyzing abilities, everyone will consider you as the most understanding and compassionate. Since you try to analyze everyone around you in such details, only you are able to observe perspectives which non-analyzers can never see. You are so concerned about overanalyzing your own behavior that you are ready to accommodate anybody, be kind to every person, and try to become a great example of considerateness.

When you're not able to comprehend something, then your brain tries hard to observe the same situation from another perspective. This is how your analysis becomes clearer. This is why you are considered as more compassionate, considerate, and tolerant.

What you learn from various viewpoints on the same situation is that there is really no perfection in life. This revelation makes you more understanding and compassionate of every person around you. People will see you as one of the kindest human beings on the planet, and in turn, you'll feel proud of your analyzing abilities.

2.) Being Great Acquaintance

Because of your ability to analyze people, they will surely consider you a great friend and acquaintance. You're always there when your friends or known people need advice on any problem. You are always available to analyze them, think with them, and since you are a great problem solver, you'll try to sort out all the problems in their life.

When your friends or family members need your advice or help, you consider this as a perfect opportunity to use your skills to help others. You analyze them by breaking down the events, thoughts, and messages to search for a perfect solution to move forward. You try to analyze and comprehend people and situations better to reach a common ground in order to minimize or avoid any conflict. This will certainly help you prosper in your personal as well as professional life.

3.) Being Selfless

Analyzing people doesn't mean that you're only doing this to gain fame. It's not true at all! Some people might think that whatever you're doing is because you don't want people to dislike you. However, you spend the time to read and analyze the behavior of other people so that you can't reverse what you know about others. You do it because you understand how to treat people well. You know, appreciate, and comprehend varying personalities and perspectives, and this ability empowers you to treat people well. This is the reason why analyzers are different beings.

4.) Being Highly Dependable

People find you highly dependable because you simply cannot disappoint anyone. As an analyzer, you would hate to disappoint anyone who comes to you for help. You're very proud of your special ability and you always try your level best to live up to desired expectations. As a result, you always try to make sure that you don't leave any stone unturned and make best efforts to sort out problems by reaching a common ground.

For instance, you do not like to keep anyone waiting for you because you don't like to wait for anyone either. So, if you are late for a get-together or meeting after you promised to reach there on time, you'll surely understand and analyze how you made others feel when you made them wait for you. Therefore, instead, you'll always reach the get-togethers or meetings ten minutes early. This virtue makes you highly reliable because people know that you'll always deliver if you promised something.

5.) Being Always Prepared

You are always prepared no matter what the settings are. Preparation is your strong point. Be it a date or a meeting or a presentation, you imagine all the directions in advance. You're always prepared for every single thing. For instance, if you have to attend a business meeting and you know about it days in advance until that meeting is over, your brain keeps on planning and strategizing the ways to tackle the meeting. If you're invited to a social gathering, even then you analyze how you can help, what to take, and what you need do to make that gathering memorable.

6.) Being Smart and Intellectual

Reading and analyzing people makes you really smart and intellectual. Your thinking pattern has attained an art form status. At this point, your brain capacities are fully stretched taking into account the fact that you work overtime with an aim to analyze and comprehend all the information in details.

Your brain never shuts-off, which means you have well-devised viewpoints on any topic or subject and you are prepared to discuss it right this moment! Driven by your ability to analyze others, you are pretty well-informed on numerous topics. This makes you skilled enough to take part in discussions dealing with any topics or subjects.

7.) Enjoy Great Relationships

You enjoy great relationships because you spend so much time analyzing your own relationship. You're always ready with a bullet-point list of how you can make your relationships better every day. You always try to set things right and as a result end up having great and healthy relationships. You partners always appreciate all the efforts you put to strengthen the relationship and you also compel them to maintain a cordial relationship.

You even remember old disagreements and always try to make determined efforts to avoid any further damage. You always try to tackle the situation in a different way to make things better for your relationship to last long. Old problems and disagreements do not easily leave your brains. But, it doesn't at all mean that you hold grudge against your partners. Such memories actually drive your analyzing ability to reach its peak and make you work hard to attain more meaningful relationship.

8.) Being Empathetic

You are very empathetic and beyond considerate. Because of your ability to analyze people you already know how people feel about you. This is why no person has more empathy than you have. As your brain is continuously searching for different options and perspectives, you're very much aware of and understand the different situations which emerge along with the multifaceted problems. You have the ability to clearly view and feel the root cause of pain and distress in a person since you're constantly reliving such experiences. These remain fresh in your memory and make you more empathic towards people.

9.) Motivating Others

You motivate others to read and analyze people. You have the power to fuel anybody's mind. People are continuously discussing, pondering, debating, and conversing. So many mental activities can make anyone take an interest in the topic you are discussing and make them join you. As a result, people consider you as great stimulator because you have the skills to drive others read, analyze and reach their own ideas, perspectives and solutions.

In spite of great advantages and benefits, people with analyzing ability are also overwhelmed by insecurities. As you keep on analyzing people, you are continuously bombarded with more and more opinions and perspectives angles, layers, and ideas which simply have no end.

You realize that in this world everyone is a winner and a loser. Sometimes people win and many times they lose. Furthermore, your analyzing abilities always drive you to improve constantly and you never attain a sense of complete gratification. However, you also have the power to realize that this situation is bound to happen. So, you can prepare yourself beforehand and keep on leveraging the benefits of a healthy, happy and better life.

Chapter 5: Body Language Defined

We define body language as a type of non-verbal communication, in which thoughts, feelings and intentions are expressed through physical cues such as eye movement, gestures, body posture, facial expressions, touch, and use of space. The use of body language to communicate is referred to as kinesics.

Though body language employs physical behaviors for expression, you shouldn't confuse it with sign language. This is because sign language corresponds to spoken language. It has its own unique grammar system in addition to exhibiting properties contained in other languages. Body language, however, doesn't have specific grammar, absolute meaning, or particular properties and is therefore interpreted broadly.

Actually, different countries, communities, and social groups all have distinct and agreed-upon interpretations of specific behaviors. Though it may not be 100% universal, body language has been proven to facilitate the majority of information that is relayed during interpersonal interactions. Body language helps develop relationships between people, even though at times it may appear ambiguous. Therefore, it demands that you try to accurately interpret a person's body language to avoid being misunderstood in social circles and situations.

Now that you understand what body language is, the subsequent steps are going to take you through everything you need to know to apply body language in your daily life. To start us off, we will discuss how to make the right first impression and how to read the first impressions that others present.

Chapter 6: History Of Body Language

Philosophers and scientists have connected human physical behavior with meaning, mood and personality for thousands of years, but only in living memory has the study of body language become as sophisticated and detailed as it is today.

Body language studies and written works on the subject are very sparse until the mid-1900s.

The first known experts to consider aspects of body language were probably the ancient Greeks, notably Hippocrates and Aristotle, through their interest in human personality and behavior, and the Romans, especially Cicero, relating gestures to feelings and communications. Much of this early interest was in refining ideas about oration - speech-making - given its significance to leadership and government.

Isolated studies of body language appeared in more recent times, for example, Francis Bacon in Advancement of Learning, 1605, explored gestures as reflection or extension of spoken communications. John Bulwer's Natural History of the Hand published in 1644, considered hand gestures. Gilbert Austin's Chironomia in 1806 looked at using gestures to improve speech-making.

Charles Darwin in the late 1800s could be regarded as the earliest expert to have made a serious scientific observation about body language, but there seems little substantial development of ideas for at least the next 150 years.

Darwin's work pioneered much ethnological thinking. Ethology began as the science of animal behavior. It became properly established during the early 1900s and increasingly extends to human behavior and social organization.

Where etiology considers animal evolution and communications, it relates strongly to human body language. Ethologists have progressively applied their findings to human behavior, including body language, reflecting the evolutionary origins of much human non-verbal communication - and society's growing acceptance of evolutionary rather than creationist theory. Austrian zoologist and 1973 Nobel Prize winner Konrad Lorenz (1903-89) was a founding figure in etiology. Desmond Morris, the author of The Naked Ape, discussed below, is an ethologist, as is the evolutionary biologist Richard Dawkins (b. 1941) a leading modern thinker in the field. Ethology, like psychology, is an over-arching science which continues to clarify the understanding of body language.

The modern and accessible study of body language as we know it today is very recent.

In his famous 1971 book 'Body Language,' Julius Fast (1919-2008) wrote: "...kinesics [body language and its study] is still so new to a science that its authorities can be counted on the fingers of one hand..."

Julius Fast was an American award winning writer of fiction and non-fiction work dealing especially with human physiology and behavior. His book Body Language was among the first to bring the subject to a mainstream audience.

Significantly the references in Julius Fast's book (Birdwhistell, Goffman, Hall, Mehrabian, Scheflen, etc. - see body language references and books below) indicate the freshness of the subject in 1971. All except one of Julius Fast's cited works are from the 1950s and 1960s.

The exception among Fast's contemporary influences was Charles Darwin, and specifically his book The Expression of the Emotions in Man and Animals, written in 1872, which is commonly regarded as the beginnings of the body language science, albeit not recognized as such then.

Sigmund Freud and others in the field of psychoanalysis - in the late 1800s and early 1900s - would have had a good awareness of many aspects of body language, including personal space, but they did not focus on nonverbal communications concepts or develop body language theories in their right. Freud and similar psychoanalysts and psychologists of that time were focused on behavior and therapeutic analysis rather than the study of nonverbal communications per se.

A different view of human behavior related to and overlapping body language, surfaced strongly in Desmond Morris's 1967 book The Naked Ape, and in follow-up books such as Intimate Behaviour, 1971. Morris, a British zoologist, and ethologist, linked human behavior - much of it concerned with communications - to human 'animalistic' evolution. His work remains a popular and controversial perspective for understanding people's reactions, and while his theories did not focus sharply on body language, Morris's popularity in the late 1960s and 1970s contributed significantly to the increasing interest among people beyond the scientific community - for a better understanding of how and why we feel and act and communicate.

An important aspect of body language is a facial expression, which is arguably one part of body language for which quite early 'scientific' thinking can be traced:

Physiognomy is an obscure and related concept to body language. Physiognomy refers to facial features and expressions which were/are said indicate the person's character or nature, or ethnic origin.

The word physiognomy is derived from medieval Latin, and earlier Greek (physiognomonic), which originally meant (the art or capability of) judging a person's nature from his/her facial features and expressions. The ancient roots of this concept demonstrate that while body language itself is a recently defined system of analysis, the notion of inferring human nature or character from facial expression is ancient.

Kinesics (pronounced 'kinesics' with stress on the 'ee') is the modern technical word for body language, and more scientifically the study of body language.

The word kinesics was first used in English in this sense in the 1950s, deriving from the Greek word kinesis, meaning motion, and seems to have first been used by Dr. Ray Birdwhistell, an American 1950s researcher, and writer on body language. (See references).

The introduction of a new technical word - (in this case, kinesics) - generally comes after the establishment of the subject it describes, which supports the assertion that the modern concept of body language - encompassing facial expressions and personal space - did not exist until the 1950s.

Proxemics is the technical term for the **personal space** aspect of body language. The word was devised in the late 1950s or early 1960s by Edward Twitchell Hall, an American anthropologist. The word is Hall's adaptation of the word proximity, meaning closeness or nearness. (See personal space.)

From the word kinesics, Ray Birdwhistell coined the term **kine** to refer to a single body language signal. This is not to be confused with the old and same word kine, meaning a group of cows. Neither word seems to have caught on in a big way, which in one way is a pity, but in another way probably makes matters simpler for anyone interested in the body language of cows.

The Greek word kinesis is also a root word of kinesthetics, which is the 'K' in the VAK ('see hear feel') learning styles model.

Kinaesthetics (also known as kinesthetics), the study of learning styles, is related to some of the principles of body language, regarding conveying meaning and information via physical movement and experience.

Body language is among many branches of science and education which seek to interpret and exploit messages and meaning from the 'touchy-feely' side of life.

For example, the concepts of experiential learning, games, and exercises, and love and spirituality at work - are all different perspectives and attempts to unlock and develop people's potential using ideas centered around kinesthetics, as distinct from the more tangible and easily measurable areas of facts, figures words and logic.

These and similar methodologies do not necessarily reference body language directly, but there are very strong inter-connections.

Bloom's Taxonomy and Kolb's Learning Styles are also helpful perspectives in appreciating the significance of kinesthetics, and therefore body language, in life and work today.

The communications concepts of NLP (Neuro-linguistic Programming) and Transactional Analysis are strictly dependent on understanding body language, NLP especially.

Chapter 7: Emotional Intelligence And

Empathy

Emotional intelligence is a skill that we all use as human beings without realizing it. It is the ability to recognize and manage your own emotions and the emotions of others around you. It means to understand the difference between feelings, what they mean and apply them to everyday life problems and situations.

Emotional intelligence, also known as EI is similar to 'empathy'. To be empathetic towards someone is putting yourself in their situation, in their shoes and feeling the emotions they are feeling. All these skills are combined in making your EI higher and in fact making you more successful and happy in life.

Everyone has that one friend who is a great listener and whatever problems they may be going through will sit and nod and give you great advice while you are a crying heap on the floor. We always also have that one friend that never gets angry or violent and controls their feelings incredibly calmly. I know for a fact we all have that one friend that is always saying, "I know how you feel" and then proceeds in a calm matter to advise you in a matter of fact manner on how to deal with your dilemma. They always seem to be the friends that have the most friends, the happiest, the most balanced and the most loved. These people go through life easily than others because they are 'wanted'; they are given help when asked because they never stop helping others. Am I right?

To be able to use your EI to the best of your ability and to use it to make your life more balanced and content there are a few things you have to understand first. Every human being is different; we all have different characteristics, different needs and different ways of handling things but there are five factors which make up a person's EI.

- Self – awareness

Being self-aware means you have control over your emotions and yourself and you don't let it get in the way of any decision making. People in general with a high EI are very self-aware and by being like this makes them think before they act which is a good quality and we should all work on as human beings.

- Self – Regulation

Being self-regulated means you can control your emotions and control the spontaneous side of you that makes you do impulsive things, another great quality to possess because it makes you a stronger person and by regulating your own emotions you can understand others better.

- Motivation

Having a high EI means you are a very motivated person whether it is personal or in the work place, being motivated in everything you do takes you to a higher level of EI which means becoming more successful in all of life's journeys.

- Empathy

Being empathetic is a skill we should all learn to use. It is skill that comes from the heart and cannot be produced by solving math's problems. You have to be open towards others, listen, learn and advise. People with more empathy generally succeed in creating long-lasting relationships, become good listeners and manage their own life well by looking at it from another point of view.

- Social skills

Having great social skills is another factor in many people with a high EI. Being able to talk in front of others with a confidence that is friendly and being able to openly speak and make others want to talk too is all about being emotionally intelligent. To have great social skills will make you more emotionally intelligent.

Emotional intelligence is in the human nature and to be able to develop it to the extent that it helps you in your life take note of the five points above. By working on them all it will open your mind and your heart up therefore making you more emotionally intelligent.

There are many ways that you can learn to be more emotionally intelligent and involved. When you meet new people do you instantly put them in a group and stereotype them? If you do, next time, take a breath and be more open to them before judging. Put yourself in their shoes and understand where they are coming from. Ask questions and listen to them, this will help you be more empathetic.

Whether it be at work or at home do you focus on your needs and praise yourself more than others? Do you look for praise all the time? Do you expect to be rewarded for the things you do? Try to step back from yourself and praise in your glory quietly and instead give praise to others, notice what others are succeeding in and be genuinely happy for them.

When you have a quiet five minutes sit down with a pen and paper and note all the things that aren't great about yourself. Look at yourself as if you were someone else and try to manage the imperfections that could be worked on. For example, do you get frustrated and give up quickly? Try to relax and focus. Working on yourself and understanding the good and bad in yourself will help you to understand others in the long run.

Write down all the times you have blamed someone else for something that actually hasn't been their fault. Look at past relationships that haven't worked and review the situation. Could you have been wrong too? Taking some of the blame and responsibility for your actions and learn to say sorry. People will be more open towards you and you will become more likeable because you can accept the fact you make mistakes, people make mistake.

Finally, before you do something, seriously considerate the ripple effect it will have. Will you hurt someone? Will your actions cause others happiness or pain? Before you say or do something, think. Taking the time to think before you act can prevent a lot of tears.

Being intelligent is important in life to succeed but being emotionally intelligent puts you a lot higher on the intelligence mark. By using your EI in everyday situations your life will become more satisfying and composed. By working on all of these ideas you will develop yourself spiritually and physically, you will become a better person and when you combine all these factors together you will reach a high EI that will aid you in life on many different levels.

Chapter 8: The Benefits Of Learning How

To Analyze People

Spending time during the holidays with my relatives is not only a time to appreciate all of the great things that life has blessed us with, but a time to reconnect and share stories. During this time, I will often stumble upon my parents updating one of my aunts about what I've been up to lately. My father will gesture for me to join the conversation. It then becomes my job to elaborate on the details of my life that my parents exaggerate. Then a weird thing happens - my aunt will start to speak to my parents in Chinese!

I couldn't tell you how many times I've found myself completely dumbfounded, hearing my parents speak to a relative in their native tongue. Growing up Chinese in the '90s in America, I never had the desire or need to speak or understand the Chinese language - with the exception of this scenario. Since then, whenever my relatives switch from English to Chinese, I've had to learn to rely on observing their tone of voice, hand gestures, and facial expressions to get a sense of what they were talking about. It was at this moment that I started to understand the value and importance of non-verbal communication.

Non-verbal communication can be defined as the communication between two or more individuals that do not require any words to convey the intended message. For example, when we smile, we are communicating that we are happy without using any words to convey this emotion. Verbal communication is any communication that involves the use of words. Experts claim that communication is 93% non-verbal and 7% verbal, which means that the majority of what we communicate about ourselves can be achieved through our body language.

Most people are so fixated on saying the right words in a job interview or on a first date that they neglect the impact of how they say these words. We place much more emphasis on verbal communication because we've been taught to read, write and speak at a very young age. Our thoughts and emotions are translated into words in order to express ourselves to others. Non-verbal communication involves expressing the exact same thoughts, but through our body language. The significant difference between the two is that our verbal communication is largely under our conscious control, while our non-verbal communication is not. For example, we can control whether we use our words to tell the truth or lie. If we haven't learned to pay attention to what our bodies are saying, our non-verbal communication can reveal the innermost thoughts and emotions that we usually hide with our words.

This book serves as a basic overview of body language analysis that will help you analyze others by extrapolating meaning from their actions. From many discussions of the subject with friends, family, and colleagues, the two most popular reasons why people develop an interest in learning how to analyze people are to figure out (1) if somebody is attracted to them and (2) if somebody is lying to them. There are two chapters on how to better assess the signals associated with both reasons, which will allow you to apply your new knowledge to real-world scenarios. And finally, the last section of the book covers how you can manage your own body language for success in your personal and professional relationships!

So take a deep breath, sit up straight and let's start analyzing people!

Chapter 9: The Benefits Of Learning How

To Analyze People

Spending time during the holidays with my relatives is not only a time to appreciate all of the great things that life has blessed us with, but a time to reconnect and share stories. During this time, I will often stumble upon my parents updating one of my aunts about what I've been up to lately. My father will gesture for me to join the conversation. It then becomes my job to elaborate on the details of my life that my parents exaggerate. Then a weird thing happens - my aunt will start to speak to my parents in Chinese!

I couldn't tell you how many times I've found myself completely dumbfounded, hearing my parents speak to a relative in their native tongue. Growing up Chinese in the '90s in America, I never had the desire or need to speak or understand the Chinese language - with the exception of this scenario. Since then, whenever my relatives switch from English to Chinese, I've had to learn to rely on observing their tone of voice, hand gestures, and facial expressions to get a sense of what they were talking about. It was at this moment that I started to understand the value and importance of non-verbal communication.

Non-verbal communication can be defined as the communication between two or more individuals that do not require any words to convey the intended message. For example, when we smile, we are communicating that we are happy without using any words to convey this emotion. Verbal communication is any communication that involves the use of words. Experts claim that communication is 93% non-verbal and 7% verbal, which means that the majority of what we communicate about ourselves can be achieved through our body language.

Most people are so fixated on saying the right words in a job interview or on a first date that they neglect the impact of how they say these words. We place much more emphasis on verbal communication because we've been taught to read, write and speak at a very young age. Our thoughts and emotions are translated into words in order to express ourselves to others. Non-verbal communication involves expressing the exact same thoughts, but through our body language. The significant difference between the two is that our verbal communication is largely under our conscious control, while our non-verbal communication is not. For example, we can control whether we use our words to tell the truth or lie. If we haven't learned to pay attention to what our bodies are saying, our non-verbal communication can reveal the innermost thoughts and emotions that we usually hide with our words.

This book serves as a basic overview of body language analysis that will help you analyze others by extrapolating meaning from their actions. From many discussions of the subject with friends, family, and colleagues, the two most popular reasons why people develop an interest in learning how to analyze people are to figure out (1) if somebody is attracted to them and (2) if somebody is lying to them. There are two chapters on how to better assess the signals associated with both reasons, which will allow you to apply your new knowledge to real-world scenarios. And finally, the last section of the book covers how you can manage your own body language for success in your personal and professional relationships!

So take a deep breath, sit up straight and let's start analyzing people!

Chapter 10: Getting To Grips With Those

Subtle Signs

In the opening chapter, I mentioned how often there will be aspects of body language that are very subtle in nature. However, thanks to this subtlety there is a very real chance that you will miss it or even underplay how you are displaying certain things yourself.

So, with that in mind, I'm going to take you through some of those key subtle signs just to make life that bit easier. Also, you can perhaps see this chapter as teaching you all about how to read body language as well since that will also prove to be rather useful in life.

The Key to Subtlety

As the word suggests, it is often the smallest of movements in body language that can tell us, or divulge, the most information. For some, this will prove to be rather depressing as they discover that they have not been able to hide their true feelings or emotions quite as well as they thought.

To help, I'm going to give you some examples of what I mean by subtle signs as that will not only make you aware of when you use them yourself, but also how to then identify them in others.

The Use of the Eyes

You have probably heard the saying that the eyes are the windows to the soul, and in body language there's no doubt that they are capable of telling you so much about what the person is thinking or feeling.

Think about this for a moment.

If you are talking to someone and you notice that their eyes are moving all over the place, how do you feel? Chances are that you perceive the individual to either be anxious or bored as they are giving off signals that are along those lines just by the way in which they are unable to maintain any sense of eye contact.

Instead, you need to make sure that you do look at individuals rather than ignoring them with your gaze as you chat. It's not only poor manners, but it's also seen as being poor body language and will give the wrong impression.

Distribution of Weight

The distribution of weight is another subtle sign that can tell you so much about an individual and what they are thinking or feeling. For example, it is accepted that the way in which you distribute your weight can send signals as to whether or not you are comfortable. An individual who is tending to put more weight on one foot than the other is sending out a signal that they are anxious and would love to be able to move away. For a positive sign, you need to plant both feet firmly, shoulders width apart, and make sure that your weight is evenly distributed as this is a more confident pose.

Your Posture

We are often told that our posture has to be good in order to prevent back issues later on in life, but there is also something else that is going on.

To display strong and confident body language, you must have good posture. For example, when sitting in a chair, you should never slouch. Also, you should not lean forward as both have the impact of making you smaller in size and is a display of anxiety.

Instead, your posture in your chair should be you sitting with your back supported, sitting tall, and yet also appearing to be relaxed.

In addition, when standing or walking, a good posture will mean you are at your full height rather than the slightly hunched over individual that most of us tend to be. Once again, you can see how walking tall with your shoulders pushed back, your neck extended to its full length will show as someone who is not afraid and confident in who they are.

Tension

Does the individual you are talking to appear to be tense in their body and even their voice? A certain rigidity in the body is generally seen as representing anxiety and fear and yet it is something that we can overlook.

What is their neck doing? How about their shoulders? Tension and nerves can often be found in these parts of the body as well as their movement.

Your Movements

Your movements can, of course, be the result of both the conscious mind as well as the unconscious mind. However, things such as the angle you are at when talking to someone can lead to certain interpretations of how you may be feeling. Always keep in mind the open and closed body language signs and how they relate to those movements. Also, even though it is accepted that strong movements represent a confident individual, there is an upper limit at which point it becomes too obvious that you are effectively trying to mask the fact that you are anxious.

Subtle signs can make a huge difference in your understanding of body language and an individual. Being aware of the smallest signs makes it easier to interpret their mood or emotions just as long as you then use that to your own advantage.

Chapter 11: Why Body Language Is

Essential For A Man To Attract A Woman

The one thing you never always hear much of in the seduction community is the value of possessing sexy and attractive body language.

A man who gives his sincere gifts to the world and understands his sincere purpose in life is considered to be a perfect man. Perfect men's also attract many of the women's in their life.

"Most people believe that they need the right thing to say, the place to go or the right strategy. Strategy is not what holds people back from searching a great relationship even though it is important in life. It's a faith system in their heads that bounds them, it's the story."

A girl would never take you seriously if you don't have a right confidence inside you. She would never ever not look at you in a venereal way and would be looking at you like someone with whom she does not want to do sex. By paying attention to your body movements, you could avoid this situation to occur.

Body language plays an important role in attracting women. You would be able to get any woman to like you lots and could have the FINEST game in the world. However, you would simply get burn and crash if you used those same successful methods in your real life and have lack of eye contact, lack of confidence etc.

To be an eye-catching among women all we need is not just have to look like Arnold Schwarzenegger, to be 007 or to drive a BMW. You need to hold something which is more important than any of those things. Something continuously projecting signals that are commanding for a romantic meeting with a woman and that is continuously with you: "The Right Body Language Of Attraction".

"The delicate signals that men put out are picked up by Women and will immediately judge if you are some fool or a potential mate".

When you enter a room, with the correct body language, you would signal the "I'm available, I'm a man, I know what I'm doing and I'm alpha" feel to every woman available there. And you can easily and quickly communicate with a woman when you have your target in your sights: "You attract me, I want to get to know you better, and I'm interested in you".

For men, it's a difficult work to point the body language symbols of a woman at the same time as we are communicating with her. On the other hand, Women are naturally appealed to the men that convey it and have got a natural technique of observing proper male by their body language. They have a cool time collecting up the vibes that show if a guy is really attractive, virtuously by how his body is interacting.

This may appear a little unbelievable, but in times like this, we are no unlike from the animal kingdom. Body language is a very essential part in human communications and shows a vital role in all the interactions.

This is why it is very essential for all of the men to know appropriate body language and to work on carrying that throughout our interactions with the people around us and women's.

Chapter 12: Academic Fields Of Body Language

Kinesics is the academic term for body language, but there is an entire spectrum of non-verbal communication each of which has their own field of study. In this chapter learn about the other types of non-verbal communication.

Motorics

Motorics, as the name implies, is the study of movement in regards to communication. This includes the sub-groups of;

Mimics – movements of the face

Pantomimics – the movement/position of the entire body

Gesture – movements of the arms and hands

There the most important point to make here is that expressions (which fall under the category of mimics) are universal.

No matter where you are in the world and what culture you are talking to, all people will interpret an expression in the same way. This provides a useful basis for communication between people of different languages or origins – let your expressions speak for you!

Oculesics

Oculescis the study or use of eye movements in non-verbal communication.

Humans have a great ability in interpreting the eye movements of other humans. We can interpret a wandering gaze as a sign of distraction or lack of interest in the current conversation.

Direct eye contact can cause a feeling of intimacy or confidence and an avoidant gaze can imply insecurity or lack of confidence. Yet conversely, at times direct eye gaze can feel inappropriate or awkward.

Eye movement can also influence the flow and control of a conversation. Changes in eye movement can be used to signal a new event which requires attention or to direct people to where we are looking.

Haptics

The study or use of physical touch in non-verbal communication.

The use of touch in non-verbal communication is incredibly complicated and nuanced. Touch can convey a vast range of emotions and intents, from playfulness to sexual attraction, to love & intimacy or even threat & violence. Touch can also be part of social convention and ritual, such as a handshake or high five.

The use of touch also varies dramatically across cultures and countries. Even within western countries, friendly touch is more common and accepted within continental Europe, as opposed to in the U.K and U.S.

Touch also varies notably across genders. Studies suggest that men interpret being touched as different than woman and are more likely to respond negatively – potentially due to implications of dominance and submissiveness.

The main take-home point of touch is that it is a very emotional method of communication, often with a greater level of intensity than other methods. If touch is used in conjunction with language and non-verbal communication, it can emphasize and reinforce the impression you make. This is a double-edged sword however – if someone is uncomfortable with your presence, or perceives you negatively, touching them will likely strengthen this perception.

Proxemics

The study and use of space in non-verbal communication. Proxemics interacts and influences haptics – you will need to be within a certain distance before touching even becomes appropriate.

If someone is standing 'too close' this can be interpreted as uncomfortable or inappropriate by the other person in the conversation. The appropriate level of closeness largely depends on the relationship between the two people involved. Study of proxemics has distinguished four approximate regions of space people can occupy in relation to another.

Intimate Distance – Less than 1.5ft

Personal Space - 1.5ft to 4ft

Social Space - 4ft to 12ft

Public Space – 12ft – 25ft

Intimate space is used for direct touch, embraces or whispering. Naturally intimate space conveys a strong and close relationship between the two people involved, often being lovers.

Personal space is typically for close friends and family. If other less familiar individuals enter this space, it is determined uncomfortable by the majority of people.

Social space is for acquaintances and other people who do not fall into the previous categories. This space is close enough to be considered reasonably engaged with the other person, but does not display any kind of intimacy or closeness.

The public space is often used for public speaking or group interactions. This is the upper bound for when conversations or verbal communication take place between people and groups.

Chronemics

The study and use of time in non-verbal communication. A fast tempo to a conversation can often be the result of anger or frustration, but it can also be as a result of engagement and excitement. Slower tempo can be the result of a lack of interest in both parties, but it can also imply that they are comfortable in each others presence. Slow tempo and pauses can often imply confidence.

Outside of conversation, the use of time also carries various connotations. In the western and east asian world, the use of time is called 'monochronic', which basically means precise or measured. Arriving exactly on time to an event is considered; being five, ten or any amount of time later is interpreted as rude (at least without reason).

Conversely, in other regions, such as Latin America or Africa, time usage is often called 'polychronic'. Broader time categories are used to signal events, such as 'morning', 'afternoon', 'dusk' and there is more wideness and variance for when a person can appear for events.

Paralanguage

The study and use of the voice in non-verbal communication. This may sound rather contradictory but paralanguage is actually hugely relevant. Psychology considers that a large factor in our communication are non-verbal (i.e not language based) aspects of our speech. This includes factors such as rhythm, intonation, speaking style and stress.

Think about your own experiences. You are more likely to engage with a person who is not speaking in a monotone and likewise, greater orators know how to alter and control the pace and emphasis of what they are saying for greater impact.

Similarly, if someones voice is cracking or shacking we will interpret what they are saying as being more emotional than if their voice were calm, even if they are saying the exact same message.

To improve your paralanguage, you will need to practice. Speakers typically train themselves by giving their speech or presentation in front of a full length mirror so they can see themselves whilst speaking. Likewise, it is common for speakers and orators to record their own speech so they can better analyze their speaking habits.

Bipedics

The study and use of foot and leg gestures in non-verbal communication. Bipedics is a relatively new addition to the other categories, with far less research on how influential it is. Nonetheless, be aware of its existence! You may hear of bipedics in the future!

As you can see, there are a lot of categories! Many of these categories overlap or cover the same conceptual space – bipedics (movement of the legs & feet) for example, can be interpreted as a sub-group of motirics (movement).

Similarly, the categories mentioned in chapter 1 will also fit into the categories (emblems for example are a type of **gesture).**

It's not crucial to appreciate the exact categorizations, but they can give you a great lead for further research and well as the striking variety of body language signals that people actually consider. Chances are, before reading this chapter you were not aware that bipedics – or the body language of the legs and hips – was a scientific field of its own accord! Yet now you know that even your legs can give influence how you are portrayed.

Chapter 13: The Pioneers Of Body

Language

The art of body language is something that began to gain worldwide traction and genuine interest of notable researchers around the early 20th century. Although there is said to be innovators who have studied this topic long before this century. Francis Bacon happened to be one of the pioneers who took a keen interest in the research of observational body language. This type of research is solely dependent upon observation and experiences as opposed to ideology or thesis. Bacon was an English theorist who happened to be a legislator and scientist, as well, who felt as if the gestures of the body were an extremely important element that had been neglected in research by prior philosophers.

Bacon was adamant that the outward gestures, hence, body language and the demeanor of an individual directly links to the state of mind of that individual. He indicated that the way a person talks, coupled with their body language assists in developing an impression of that person's character.

King James, I was another distinguished philosopher who was the initial investigator of facial gestures. His saying, "As the tongue speaketh to the ear so the gesture speaketh to the eye," speaks massively when influencing naysayers that facial expressions are indeed a silent language that speaks volumes when deciphered accurately.

Charles Darwin was also a philosopher who, like King James I, took a very special interest in the way people expressed emotions in their faces. Darwin is noted for performing one of the first research studies in determining how people distinguish emotion in their face. Darwin's belief was that facial muscles operated in unison to produce a few broad facial expressions. In order to test what he believed to be true, Darwin organized a study in which he displayed eleven random slides of individuals showing various facial expressions. The people who were participants in the study were to convey what emotion they felt the person in each picture slide exhibited.

Darwin's research ultimately concluded that in regards to common emotions such as happiness, sadness, fear, and anger the results were unanimous and every respondent was in agreeance. Darwin went on to write a book in 1872 entitled, "The Expressions of Emotions in Man and Animals," which included the results of the facial expression study conducted.

Chapter 14: You're Hired! Now What?

What if you're gainfully employed but you're just spinning your wheels in the company? You're not getting promoted; no one seems to take notice of you or your contributions; and you're starting to wonder if anyone would even notice if you didn't show up for work.

Meanwhile, your coworker — let's call him Stan — is rocketing his way up the corporate ladder. Before you start throwing accusations around (even in your own mind), take an (inconspicuous) look at Stan's body language. Maybe you could learn a thing or two from him.

I'm a Pro

You might think you're a better person than Stan, and you may be right. But being nicer doesn't get you ahead in the business world — being the better worker does. And sometimes you don't even have to be the better worker; you just have to know how to project the image of being the better worker.

Again, this goes back to showing your confidence and a positive attitude. Walk tall. Sit straight. Know how to look like you're listening to others. Cultivate a professional handshake. Look other people in the eye. Smile. All of these body language cues make you look interested and approachable — like someone who's willing to jump in and help at any opportunity. Chances are, Stan knows how to display these characteristics without looking like a phony. He looks like he knows what he's doing, so other people assume he does.

I'm a Con

What kind of body language hurts you in the office? Any actions that make you look abrasive, unsure, or uninterested, such as:

- **Poor posture**
- **Bad eye contact**
- **Weak handshake**
- **Any nervous gestures, like handwringing or foot jiggling**

Now, take another look at Stan. He stands tall, he makes a point of making eye contact with people, he shakes hands like he's running for the Senate …

Can you see the difference? Stan looks like a port in a storm, like the guy you can run to if something goes wrong in the office. The worker who never makes eye contact and shies away from other people with his body language is going to go unnoticed at all times, including times of crisis, which is when leaders are made (and later promoted).

Now here's the important part: Given two equal job performances, a boss is likely to promote the person he likes better. And it's probably easier to like someone like Stan, because he gives everyone ample opportunity to see him making his impressive way through the office. It's not fair, but it happens all the time. You have to know how to play Stan's game if you want to get ahead in your workplace.

Walking Disasters

There's body language that will get you promoted, body language that will get you ignored, and body language that will get you fired. Everyone knows that some motions — like obscene gestures of any sort — are flat-out inappropriate in the workplace. But there are some body language cues that fall into gray areas. Technically, they aren't offensive, but there's something about them that makes other people uncomfortable. These may include things like:

- **Prolonged eye contact**
- **Excessive use of the hands to emphasize a point**
- **Excessive sighing or throat clearing**
- **Round-the-clock frowning**
- **Lingering touches**

Now, the last item on the list may actually fall into a legal area, depending on who's doing the touching and where. The other actions, however, might be perceived as just ... kind of creepy. You know these things when you see them — the coworker who never looks away (or even blinks) while he's talking to you; the coworker who flaps her arms like wings when she's excited about something; the person who always looks angry (and whom you're afraid to ask a question of).

Again, the successful employee gets along well with everyone in the office and appears eager to jump into any project or problem. This isn't to say that someone who doesn't know about appropriate eye contact is a bad person, but he may make other people nervous, which in turn may result in coworkers avoiding him.

For better or for worse, body language has a marked effect on interactions in the business world. It's a dog-eat-dog world out there, but you don't have to join in the backstabbing and gossiping that go on in far too many offices in order to get promoted. By learning to carry yourself as a true professional (someone who isn't afraid of what the day may throw your way), you make a distinct impression on the people around you, including your bosses. Stand tall, shake firmly, and make eye contact, no matter how foreign these actions seem to you at first. No one remembers a wallflower — use your body language to make yourself visible, memorable, hire-able, and promotable.

Those Pesky Palms Again

You'll remember from earlier that palms up is a friendly gesture; palms down indicates a closed-off speaker who isn't open to new ideas.

Someone who offers his hand to you with his palm facing down is telling you that he's the top dog in the office. This is the kind of move that the president of the company might use when meeting with underlings. If someone offers you his hand in a palm-down position, it's all right to offer yours vertically … and wait for him to shake your hand (unless he's your boss). The funny thing is that some particularly aggressive people will take your hand and try to turn it palm up as they shake it. Go ahead and fight the twist, and don't feel a bit strange about the wrist wrestling you're engaging in. You're simply protecting your own standing.

Is it wrong to offer your hand in a palm-up manner? Not if you're supremely confident and/or in a position of power to begin with. This is actually seen as something of a humbling move and will most likely make others feel more comfortable in your presence.

Other Shaky Touches

You've seen brothers and male friends shake each other's hands and simultaneously clap each other on the shoulder — obviously, a way of saying, "I'm so glad to see you!" Is this motion reserved for personal meetings? If your boss smacks you on the shoulder, is that a way of saying he really likes you, or is it a way of saying something else entirely?

The shoulder smack, along with the elbow grab, is almost always simply an extension of goodwill. It's a way of expressing genuine happiness at seeing the other person without moving into hug territory (though sometimes the shoulder clap is a prelude to the hug, especially among male family members or friends).

When to Give In

The one situation where you should give in to the other person's whims is when you're shaking hands with your boss. If he has a longer shake than you, just hang back and let him take the lead.

Here's a subtle move that often follows the handshake and is easy to miss: Let's say you're finishing up a meeting with a colleague. You shake hands and as you turn to walk out the door, he walks with you, putting his hand on your shoulder. This is a condescending move, one that suggests that you're the underling in this situation.

If you work with someone who is prone to the condescending shoulder touch, move out of his range after shaking his hand. When he does this to you, it feeds his own perception that he's higher up on the ladder than you are, so to speak, which may not mean anything in the real world ...

but there's no sense feeding this guy's ego.

You may not be bothered by the shoulder touch, but you don't want the other person to start believing that he has some sort of control over you. You want him to know that you're a force to be reckoned with when push comes to shove. Steering clear of his attempts at intimidation is a great way to get this message through loudly and clearly.

You, On Display

Presentation. The very word can kickstart born talkers, while striking nothing short of terror into the hearts of their less gregarious counterparts. People who hate to talk in front of others often mitigate the effect of their poor presentation skills by saying, "I'm a hard worker; that should be worth something" or, "I'll let the work speak for itself."

In small companies, it may be that simple — everyone knows everyone well and, more importantly, your boss is more likely to know that you do work hard every day.

In larger companies, though, presentations are often the only time your boss — and her bosses — are able to see what you've been up to.

Keep It Hidden!

Why do you want to keep your work under wraps until the last second? Once the audience sees the work, they aren't listening to you anymore — they're judging whatever is on the easel, the table, the screen, or the wall. It's just human nature to do this. So before you show them anything, you want to use effective body language to set up the story behind the work.

You know what that means? It's show time! Even if you loathe presenting your work, there are a few moves you can make during any presentation that will make you appear more relaxed and comfortable. And sometimes that's all you need to feel relaxed and comfortable.

Start by knowing the room and where you can hang or position your report, your ad, your art, or whatever it is you're showing off. The work should be behind you, and if possible, it should not be revealed until you've had a chance to talk your audience through it.

Start with a story that has some tie to the work — maybe it's how this idea came into existence, the research, an anecdote related to the research, but something that any human being could relate to. Now, use body language to relate to your audience. How, you're asking?

- Make eye contact with several people in the room. This can be tough if the bigwigs are there, and if they make you nervous, then seek out a couple of friendly faces first — but do make sure to make eye contact with the big bosses.

- Move. It's hard enough to get up in front of a room of people — now you're expected to walk around? Yes. Now, you don't have to make circles around the conference table; you can simply take a couple of slow steps back and forth every now and then. This isn't meant to make you look hyper; the point is not to plant your feet in one spot for too long, because you'll come off looking like a scarecrow.

- Use your arms and hands. Again, this is a move that helps you appear comfortable. Imagine how you speak to your friends when you're explaining something — you probably use some form of hand gestures. Go ahead and do the same thing here — just keep it slow and mellow (in other words, no karate chops) so you don't startle anyone.

- Know the work. When you're actually presenting your work, you shouldn't be totally fixated on it — you should appear to be intimate enough with it that you can continue making eye contact with those in the room (to some degree).

- Show excitement. It's hard to buy into a presentation when the speaker looks as though he's being tortured, so try to appear content and confident when you have the floor. If you're interested in the work, other people will be interested, too.

Play the Game and Play It Well

We've all seen people who are less talented than their coworkers earn big promotions. Naturally, peers and colleagues are left scratching their heads. How is it possible that this person who was barely qualified for the position he was in has risen to a position he truly doesn't deserve?

Well, this person, while perhaps unfit to perform the job he was hired to do, probably plays the office game and plays it well — and a big part of that game involves body language. Chances are he is a master at projecting a positive attitude, a happy demeanor, and knows exactly where and when to place himself so it appears he's involved in more than he is. And just as important, he knows how to keep out of the petty office politics.

Though it kills us to admit it, he's doing something right — something that the rest of us could learn from. Try these body language tricks to portray a positive outlook around the office, and see what happens.

- Look interested in meetings, even if you feel the topic is a waste of your time. Sit up straight, open your eyes, and make eye contact with whoever is speaking. Assume there is interest in what is going to be said and look as if you are in fact interested.
- Make yourself more visible. Pipe up and ask questions in meetings — speakers and employers love to know that people are listening and interested.
- Be friendly and happy. Take the time to smile when you say hello to people. When people engage you in conversation, tilt your head to the side, make eye contact, and nod every now

and then — you'll win tons of allies just by looking like you're a good listener.

- Lose the meekness. Stand up straight and use a confident stride when you're passing through the office. It's all right to look like you know exactly what you're doing, even if you don't.

- Don't let anyone look down on you — literally. Let's say someone stops by your desk to give you instructions on a project and this is clearly going to take several minutes. Invite that person to sit, or stand to be at their eye level. The person who is physically highest in a conversation is deemed dominant.

One caveat: If you're trying to win a promotion, this is not a one-day commitment; it's a cubicle-lifestyle change. But don't worry. For one thing, you can bite your tongue all day long, and for another, once you leave the office, you can let it all hang out.

Everyone is under pressure in this current economy. Employees are doing more work for the same — or less — money, and employers are just trying to keep the lights on and the doors open. A positive attitude (even if you're just pretending) can go a long way toward showing that you get what your boss is up against and you're the person to help him lead the way to unimaginable success.

Chapter 15: How To Improve Nonverbal Communication☐

Ensure to manage stress at the moment

Your ability to communicate is compromised when stressed making you likely to misread other people, lapse in to unhealthy knee patterns of behavior or send confusing or off-putting nonverbal signals. Being upset can make others upset too hence worsening the situation as emotions are contagious. Whenever stressed during a conversation, calm down and regain your emotional equilibrium, so that you are better equipped to deal with the situation in a positive way. Employ your senses of touch, hearing, smell and taste to find out the fastest and sure way to calm down.

Develop emotional awareness

You need to be aware of your emotions and how they influence you in order to send accurate nonverbal cues. You should also recognize and beware of others true feelings and why they are sending their cues. This helps you to accurately read, create trust and respond positively to your listeners.

Watch yourself, and others

Ensure to focus on the use of your body so as to increase the expressive nature appropriately with minimal drama. In meetings and presentations, gestures are often and failing to match nonverbal communication with words, people opts to listen with their eyes since the nonverbal message is always more accurate.

Face people

Look at the people you are communicating with and face them head on, instead of giving them silent glances.

Maintaining eye contact.

While speaking with anyone, especially co-workers, superiors or direct reports, eye contact is very crucial. When you try to increase eye contact while speaking with others, find out if they are making and maintaining it with you. It shows that you are open and communicative and overdoing it makes you seem creepy. Sensing discomfort or dishonesty comes when the person avoids eye contact and you should try asking questions in order to ease the discomfort and enhance communication.

Work on body posture

A nonverbal indicator of confidence level is indicated by your body posture, that is the ability to express yourself while standing up straight and avoiding slouching in your chair. A postural shift involves the movement of your body as a whole while conveying a message using one part of the body is gesturing. A closed personality and lack of confidence is indicated by a closed posture (crossed legs and folded arms) while an open posture is a much more confident pose (arms spread in a relaxed manner). In order o avoid sending mixed messages, the posture should be in sync with the messages. You need to sit up straight and avoid slumping since it conveys disinterest and inattention. Being bored is displayed by rocking back and forth in your chair or leaning back while active interest in both the person and conversation is demonstrated by leaning forward when listening to someone speak.

Smile

It is universal across countries and cultures especially in informal situations. Smiling to your audience sends a message that you are open to a two-way dialogue, and approachable. Whenever you want pick side in a debate or saying something controversial, smiling can help you win people to your cause.

Straighten your desk

A message that you are careless or disorganized is eminent with a floppy desk or office. The symptom of a larger problem like inefficiency is portrayed by messy desks, which stems from inability to find important papers and files. You have to be organized to reduce stress and improve productivity. Stop creating vertical files on your desk and rely on to-do files that can be kept in drawers.

Sit up straight and shake hands firmly

This is to show you are serious, confidant and professional. It counts a lot for first impressions and also helps you to pay more attention to the conversation at hand.

Brush up your appearance

Ahead of public speaking and engagements or big presentations make yourself look beautiful. It symbolizes you take care of yourself and pay attention to details. It also prepares you for the task at hand and gives a little confidence.

Respect personal space

Take a lead from the people you are talking to create the different amount of space they need. If they keep a wide berth and like to have a big space, don't push them outside their comfort zone by getting up in their face. You should also prepare to do the same if they are happy to get close and personal.

Pay attention

While speaking to anyone, pay as much attention as possible. Ensure also to minimize distractions as much as possible in order to focus solely on your conversation. This makes people feel they are very important and hence a positive audience.

Read your audience

You have to be aware of your audience nonverbal communication if you are making a presentation. Beware of signs of yawning, dozing off, slouching which means you have lost their attention. On the other hand, if the group is interested and energized, the body language may convey that they want you to ask for their input and thoughts. As a manger and speaker, enhance your abilities by learning to read your audience mood.

Listen to your voice

The various fluctuations in one's voice like the pitch, tone, inflection, rhythm and volume are involved in paralinguistic, or paralanguage. They have a powerful effect on communication, for example, a loud or forceful tone conveys a stronger or more serious message unlike softer tones. In a workplace, sarcasm can also create problems. Stress is caused by a manager's sarcastic tone since his (joking) tone is meant to contradict his words (biting or hurtful).

Match other people

Adapt your body language to suit your listeners by keeping an eye to what they are doing while talking to them. If they lean towards you, do the same and if they are gesturing rapidly, follow suit. Remember not to copy negative body language like fiddling, frowning or crossing your arms.

Question yourself

Monitor yourself throughout the day and ask yourself how you were perceived at the meeting. Could you have done something differently? Were people really interested on what you were saying, did they pay attention? Did you listen well to others? Your self-awareness increases as you answer these questions.

Practice

Practice makes perfect, and by practicing, you will be improving. You can film yourself and watch it back looking for any potential pitfalls. Watching it on the mute gives a fuller idea of what you are expressing, out oy the words you are saying. To be ready when you are called upon, you need to keep practicing and improving.

All these tips are useful and truly speaking they will help you engage your audience and hold their interest. Some people are more aware of slight distinctions of body language communication than others and adding up an extra dimension during speeches and presentations can help us make dramatic improvements in our ability to communicate effectively.

Chapter 16: Spotting Deception

It's not only inside the office that the need to spot deception arises. For managers and employers, this skill is quite beneficial. However, our modern economy is filled with threats, often caused and brought upon by fellow human beings. Reading through lies, dishonesty and deception can actually save us from trouble and wasting hard-earned money.

With the onset of different products and services (such as real estate, beauty and health products, insurance, etc.) that are available for sale, we sometimes find ourselves falling into a scam without knowing it. Salespeople will blast self-confidence so effectively and wear the best suits so fashionably that an innocent person would immediately invest trust in everything they say, only to find out later that they are scammers.

Another scenario where lie spotting can play a role is with friends and even with a significant other. Friends come and go, especially for a person with a very active social life. Some will enter and even force their way to your life with a motive. Though it may not be a bad intention, it's best to know if there are any to avoid surprises or to be able to defend oneself from the possibility of trouble. As for a significant other, knowing if she's hiding secrets can be helpful. She could be planning to move out or break-up, or worse, she could be cheating.

For whatever purpose it may serve, learning how to spot lies can be a necessity.

What to look for in Facial Expressions

Remarkably, the human face is capable of exhibiting 10,000 different expressions out of its 43 muscles. Thankfully, knowing all of them is not necessary to spot deception. The best thing about the face is that not all of its expressions can be controlled and it often reveals a person's genuine feelings or thoughts – making it easier to spot lies. Below are some general guidelines when reading a person's face to uncover dishonesty.

The Power of Symmetry☐

As discussed in the first chapter, facial expressions can be grouped to six general emotions, namely happiness, fear, surprise, anger, sadness and disgust. Thanks to the extensive study by Paul Ekman, he proved that our faces express these symmetrically. When the face muscles move in accordance to these emotions, both sides exhibit or reveal the corresponding feeling. Therefore, asymmetrical facial expressions indicate a lie. For example, if a surprise for a colleague at work is revealed and only one side of his face shows the signs of shock, chances are he already knew about it.

Spotting Micro-Expressions

This, by far, is the most difficult skill to develop. The reason why these expressions are tagged as "micro" is because they flash very briefly across the face – 1/25th of a second to be precise. Genuine emotions always instantly appear, and it takes a split-second before a person can consciously or subconsciously neutralize them. These are the best giveaways to know if an individual is lying or hiding something. However, detecting these will take practice and extensive knowledge in body language, especially facial expressions.

Smiles and Eyes

Genuine smiles involve both the upper and lower portions of the face. Of course, the mouth plays a big part in this. However, deciphering whether it's true or fake depends on the upper. There is such a term as "smiling eyes" because an honest smile has them. When the eyes narrow and lines (or "crow's feet" as some may call it) appear at the sides, it's a true smile. The best way to practice scrutinizing one from the other is by looking at selfies and candid photos (those that feature a laughing or smiling person).

Try covering the bottom half of the face in these pictures, and focus on the expression of the upper half. If happiness can be felt or seen in the eyes, it's genuine. On the other hand, if it seems neutral, then the smile is not genuine. Therefore, if a lover's smile didn't touch the top half of her face (or if only one side exhibited the emotion) upon asking if she's alright, she's probably not and she's hiding it from you.

Sadness is Reflected in the Chin

It is easy to angle the sides of the mouth downward when faking sadness. However, it is nearly impossible to keep the chin from moving. When a person exhibiting this emotion is insincere, there will always be extra chin movement.

Maintained Eye Contact

It is common belief that when a person cannot maintain eye contact, he is lying. However, even when stating completely honest words, a person still has the

125

tendency to look away or down. In fact, it is when an individual maintains or stretches eye contact that one should be wary because liars believe that if they do this, their story would be believed in. Many are serving jail time because they have been wrongfully convicted by the jury for the simple reason they were not able to maintain eye contact. The direction the eyes look often bears varied meanings, and it does not always denote insincerity. These meanings will be further explained in the following chapter.

What to note in Body Language

It has been discussed in the earlier chapters of this book that body language contributes most to effective communication. However, many of us rely heavily on verbal expressions and word use to get the desired message and emotions across when, in fact, we should rely most on our body signals. The same goes with liars. They tend to practice their lines and control their tone when expressing a statement, but seldom do they master their gestures.

Inconsistencies are often the giveaway when observing both verbal and nonverbal signals. What the liar says might not match how he acts. The following are some body signals and signs that may denote insincerity.

1. Head

Fabricating a story takes up much of a person's attention and focus that there is a high probability that he would be unable to match the movements of his head with his words. A liar may say "no," but his head will reflexively nod when lying to a question.

2. Face

The stress of lying increases tension and the person will automatically and unconsciously relieve this by constantly touching his face. A liar may touch his neck, throat and mouth, or scratch his nose or behind the ear.

3. Shoulders

Much like in facial expressions, asymmetry in shoulder gestures denotes deception. We can express varied emotions and thoughts through this underrated body part, such as exasperation when it drops, discomfort when it hunches up, or "I don't know" or "I don't care" when it shrugs. Genuine gestures are complete and symmetrical. Both shoulders either rise or fall when expressing honest feelings. If a person, however, moves just one side when answering a question, he is being dishonest or pretending.

4. Torso

The body tends to be more animated when telling a story. A person leans forward when emphasizing a point, and leans back when concluding a part. When someone narrating an account, on the other hand, looks and feels awkward, and hand gestures are limited and confined within a certain space, take precaution. Stiffness can denote fabrication because liars tend to freeze to avoid exposing too much emotive body language. Another clue would be when the body is not facing the accuser directly, because of the discomfort the guilty one feels.

5. **Arms**

In conjunction to the previous number, the underuse of hands during a conversation is a big clue in spotting lies, especially if the person crosses them. This is a defensive posture, and the individual may be keeping himself locked because of the thought he might leak clues to his deception. Open arms with the palms out is the opposite of this gesture and this denotes truthfulness and honesty.

6. **Hands**

Much like the arms, when the person keeps their hands in one place or limits their actions, he could be stating deceitful words. People narrating a genuine story tend to use their hands to embellish their account; if a person doesn't, there's a huge chance he himself is not invested in his statements. Other clues would be closed first or folded palms (this indicates restraint), or when the liar exaggerates the size or placement of something with his gestures.

7. Legs

This body part can reveal much information about a person's state of mind because these are harder to consciously control. When someone unusually broadens his stance, this could mean he is asserting dominance – a defensive mechanism when a person feels weak. Another sign is when the person rubs his thighs. This is an action that releases tension. In the presence of higher authority (this applies more appropriately in an office setting), an employee could splay his legs as a display of territory – another defensive posture.

8. Ankles

Locked ankles when seated or reclined is a display of anxiety. Despite looking and sounding calm, a person feels discomfort when he does this gesture. Standing during a conversation, on the other hand, with crossed ankles indicates high mental activity.

9. **Feet**

Where the feet points is usually the direction where the person want to go. If it's directed at the door, then he could be dying to leave the room. Another indication of nerves is when an individual taps his foot. This, however, may or may not imply deception or dishonesty. Gestures made by this body part should be considered with other signs to produce a viable conclusion.

10. **Space**

Setting-up physical barriers is a person's initial response when threatened, especially when he is hiding something. These can take the form of a bag, a book, or a coffee cup, and they are placed between the interrogator and the interviewee. Much like how a guilty person would sit in the farthest chair, this act is to increase his "safety zone." When suspecting deception, the best way to react to this gesture is by removing the objects.

Verbal and Nonverbal Contradictions

For this section of the book, discussions will be mixed with a brush-up of verbal inconsistencies. Focusing solely on body language in this chapter may result to false suspicions.

Lies aren't only shown in body language, but also in the manner of speaking. Disparity between these two is the best indicators of deception. A dishonest person is so focused on altering his words that he often leaves his gestures unattended, thus revealing his true feelings and intentions.

Emotions vs. Words vs. Gestures

True feelings are simultaneously expressed by words, facial expressions and gestures. For example, a surprised person would exhibit the emotion in her face, raise her hands to her mouth, and express the words "Oh my gosh!" all at the same time. However, if one of these is delayed, the person could be faking her emotion. When asking someone if his food is delicious for instance, and he replied "I love it!" but the smile came after instead of together, he is not completely invested in his statement.

Expression vs. Statements

If an ex-girlfriend of yours forced you to watch a recent trilogy about vampires, you'd know exactly what this contradiction means. Insincere words are accompanied by off facial expressions. For example, the leading lady of the said movie stated, "Why can't you see how perfectly happy I am?" but her face didn't show any trace of it – in fact, she looked stressed – she's not feeling happy at all. Another good case would be when a girl says a simple "I love you" while frowning, there's a huge chance she might not or she herself is questioning the statement.

3. **Timing**

The pace of emotions is erratic when a person is being dishonest. Emotions are either delayed, expressed longer than normal, suddenly stopped, or a combination of all three.

4. Limited

Much like how smiling with the eyes work, emotions are expressed by the whole face. Expressions of a liar, on the other hand, are limited to the mouth.

Keep in mind that observing a person exhibiting these signs may not always mean they are being deceptive. As discussed in the first chapter, a gesture can be influenced by a number of factors, and these have to be taken into consideration before making any conclusions.

Chapter 17: Common Body Language

Mistakes

Below you will find a list of the most common body language mistakes.

1. Avoiding eye contact

Avoiding eye contact might make other people presume you are a liar or simply see it as a lack of respect. Either way it is not very good.

2. Slouching

Slouching suggests that you have low self-esteem or that you are extremely tired. Slouching also reveals boredom to other party. No one wants to be seen in this light, so if you slouch, stop slouching!

3. Weak handshake

A sloppy handshake makes it seem like you are passive. A to firm handshake will have people thinking you are over aggressive. Find the perfect balance and stick with it.

4. Folding arms

Folding arms can shut you off from the rest of the world. Folding your arms can give off the impression of being closed off; it may also give the impression to others that you are not interested in what they have to say. No one wants to talk to a person who seems to be closed off, so just be yourself and relax a bit.

5. Looking down

Looking down can hint at you being self-conscious. It can also mean you are anxious. By looking down you are making yourself look inferior, so stand up with your chin held high.

6. Fidgeting

Fidgeting can show anxiety or discomfort. It may also show boredom. So if you are in a professional setting try not to fidget that much. It might make you look unprofessional.

7. Checking the clock

This one is pretty much self-explanatory. If you are glancing at the clock every second while someone is trying to engage with you it comes off as rude and arrogant.

8.   Frowning

Frowning indicates sadness and disagreement. It is okay to be sad, just try to not let affect your personal life. If you happen to disagree with something that has been said speak your mind.

Rolling your eyes☐

Rolling your eyes indicates a lack of respect and childishness. It may be a bad habit but it is necessary to get it in check as soon as possible. Especially, if you do not want someone rolling their eyes at you. Nor do you want to give off the air of being disrespectful and childish.

If you stand to close to someone it shows that you have no respect for their personal space.

Avoiding or fixing these mistakes will lead you on path to having stronger relationships.

Chapter 18: Flirting With Body Language

Everyone enjoys the art of flirting, and though the people may not really own up to the fact that they are flirting. You are able to easily see the signs of flirting if you are open to seeing it. If you find yourself displaying these body language signs or someone is displaying them towards you, then you know there is a sign of attraction.

Eye Contact

When a person is flirting with you, then he or she is going to make eye contact more often than other people. It is their way of offering the sign that they are interested. Also, when you are talking to a friend or coworker, they may keep throwing some glances toward you. That is why eye contact is one of the largest of signs when it comes to flirting.

Attempts to Get Attention

It is simple, if you like someone then you will want the attention from them. That is why someone who is interested in you will try to catch your attention. Things that are included in this is things like dressing nicer, pulling silly stunts to make you laugh, and even wearing cologne or perfumes.

Alpha Male

All men hope to be the alpha male. If they are not the alpha male, they will pretend to be. It is because it is assumed that women like the macho men. If you are female and you notice a male cracking jokes on other men in your presence or a strut, then he is into you.

Arched Eyebrows

Arched eyebrows are on the top when it comes to flirting body language. When a person speaks to you and you see them slightly raise their eyebrows, then it is no doubting that they are interested in you.

Private Space Invaded

A person that is interested in you will invade your personal space. At first it will be by "accident". It is done to test the waters on whether or not you would be repulsed if they touched you. At times this is unintentional; however it can also be done consciously.

Talks Differently

When people are flirting they will use a different tone or even style of speaking to the person they are flirting with. It will be slightly different, of even tremendously different.

Preening

Men are pretty vain naturally and one of the most obvious signs that a man is flirting is the constant preening when they are around a female that they are interested in. However, girls do this as well. The male or female will continuously make sure that their appearance is right. He or she will smooth their hair; straighten their clothes, and other small personal grooming to keep looking great for the person that they are interested in.

Facing the Body

When talking to a person of interest a male or female will shift their entire body towards them. The head, legs, knees, and their feet will be facing the person that they are interested in. It shows that they have eyes for that person and no one else.

Tilting the Head

Have you ever noticed that males slightly tilt their head when they are interested in a female? This is not done on purpose. However, it is a sure bet that they are into the person they are tilting their head at.

Touching

When a person is interested in another person they will typically touch them. The touches are gentle and subtle. At times it could be brushing or touching your arm gently or guiding you by your arm or your hand while you both are walking.

Watch the Actions

When a person is around a person that they are interested in they will normally get a bit fidgety. If you notice that a female or male seems to be fidgety around you, then it is more than likely that they are interested in you.

Laughing

Most people laugh or even giggle when they see or hear something that is funny. However, when a person is around their interest, then they will seem to laugh a lot easier. The person may act in a silly manner to catch and keep your attention.

Staring

Normally it is creepy or weird if someone is staring at another person; however, when a person has interest in another they may stare a little bit or glance at that person throughout the day. It is a very big sign of interest.

Always Around

When a guy is interested, he will typically find different opportunities to be around the person of interest. If you find that you are running into him a lot, then it is probably that he is trying to find opportunities to be around you.

Protectiveness

When a person is interested they will be a little bit more protective over their interest than others. From helping you navigate through a crowded area to other helpful actions, this shows that they are interested.

Keeping Eyes on You

If someone is interested in you, then you will notice that they are always paying attention to you. If you find that other people are trying to engage in conversation with that person and they keep their eyes on you, then it is a for sure sign that they are definitely into you.

A Touch of Jealousy

Although jealously is a grey area from healthy to non, it can be a sign that a person is interested in you if they are paying attention to your conversations with the opposite sex. They may seem annoyed or a little bit jealous. It is quite obvious that they are into you.

Chapter 19: The Essence Of A Deal

A need for an agreement begins when one party has something that another party needs. A car salesman, for instance, has an inventory of cars that car buyers need. In this case, the exchange process is simple. The buyer just needs to put up the money to get the car or sign up for a financing plan to pay for the car with future income.

The process of negotiating becomes more difficult to deal with when the assets that are being exchanged do not have a predetermined value.

For example, in a labor case, the union of workers usually refuse to work in protest. The company in question usually wants their workers to go back to work. For that to happen, its management should meet the terms that the union offers.

In some cases, however, it is impossible for a company to meet the terms of the union without risking getting broke. In this case, each party has a different assessment of the value of the assets being exchanged. The only way for both parties to reach an agreement is if one or both adjust their terms for completing the deal.

Both parties need to arrive at an agreement where the company is not financially crippled and the union's terms partially satisfied. The negotiators from each side should reach a compromise. In the end, even if neither of the two parties was completely satisfied with the deal, the negotiation ensures that each will reap their own benefits.

An Unfair Deal

When the negotiation skills of one of the representatives of the parties are below average, both parties will end up getting an imbalanced deal. This type of deal gives one of the parties a greater advantage.

In a sales arrangement, for example, an inexperienced buyer may end up buying a product at a price more expensive than its actual value. This results from the salesperson's superior knowledge of the product, the market, and the buyer's mind.

You do not want at the losing end of this kind of deal. If possible, you want to get the better part of the deal.

Set Your Non-Negotiables

In each deal, the other side will try to tip the scales in their favor. A buyer of a property, for instance, may push their luck by lowballing the price. A complainant in a case may ask for an extremely high settlement amount.

These are just a couple of examples of how people try to push their luck in the negotiating table. You will be able to avoid being on the losing side of the deal by setting your non-negotiables and sticking to it.

Non-negotiables refer to the parts of your terms that you are not willing to compromise. One example of this is setting a minimum price for your products. By setting a minimum price, you are telling the buyers that you are willing to let go of the deal if you are haggled too much. This brings us to our next point:

Be Willing to Walk Away

Before sitting down at the negotiating table, you should set a mindset that you are willing to walk away from the deal if your non-negotiable terms are not met. You will be in a bad position in a deal if the other party senses that you are unable to walk away from a deal.

In this case, people usually end up taking bad deals just to get the negotiation over with. By thinking and showing that you are willing to let go of the deal, you will force the other party to compromise.

You can show that you are willing to walk away from the deal by mentioning that you have other options. When buying a car, for example, tell the salesperson that you already visited another car lot and that you found a few that you already like. You can also say that you are there to check if they have a better offer.

By stating that you have other options, you are indirectly stating that you will walk away from the deal if the offers they have do not satisfy your needs.

Chapter 20: Tips On How To Conduct

Yourself During Interviews

When being interviewed for a job offer, or when meeting potential clients for the first time, you should:

•Always be prompt, well-dressed and have a ready smile for the interviewer. This shows energy, which can also be translated to being eager when it comes to the workplace.

•Dress well. Often, the interviewer takes into account how well put together you are during the first time you meet. Choose conservative business suits every time. Interviewers will perceive you as a team player when you do. You can always switch to more vibrant colors or designs after you get the job. When in doubt, go for solid colors like black or red. Both colors convey strength and adaptiveness.

•Do your homework beforehand. Read up as much as possible about the company you are applying in, and what the job description entails. Develop possible questions that the interviewer might ask and practice your answers extensively so that these sound natural, but not overly confident or arrogant.

•When meeting your interviewer for the first time, shake hands with a firm but not a bone-crushing grip. Pump his/her hand only twice or thrice. Never grab with both your hands, or pull the person towards you.

•Always stand or sit upright. As much as possible, occupy as much space as possible with an open posture. This conveys confidence and even fearlessness. However, always present a pleasant face so as not to give off the aura of intimidation.

•Maintain eye contact at all times. Looking all over the room during the interview gives off the impression that you are not a trustworthy person. Constantly looking up or down means that you are uncomfortable with the questions and may be hiding something that the interviewer might not like.

Other "tells" interviewers use are:

•Scratching your head or other body parts (denotes confusion.)

•Touching or rubbing your nose, mouth or chin (denotes irritation.)

•Shifting through notes instead of answering outright (denotes lack of preparation.)

•If you are right-handed, and your eyes unconsciously roll to the right and vice-versa for left-handed people. (denotes lying.)

•Avoiding any form of unnecessary gestures like fidgeting with your clothes, swinging your hair in an arc to remove a stray lock, playing with your pen, shuffling papers, etc. Not only do these actions irritate the interviewer to no end, but these are also indications that you are restless, terrified, and want the interview to end as soon as possible.

Chapter 21: Arms Body Language

Arms serve as defensive barriers when you put them across your body. On the other hand, when in open positions, it indicates feelings of security and openness, especially when used in combination with open palms. Arms are a very reliable indicator of feeling and mood, especially when combined with other body language signals. Here is an illustration of how signals combine:

*Crossed arms is possibly defensive

*Crossed arms with crossed legs is possibly defensive

*Crossed arms with crossed legs and frowning plus clenched fists is definitively defensive and possibly hostile as well. This might seem obvious in paper, but it is not always so visible when you are preoccupied with other matters. Body language involves more than simply knowing the theory: you have to be constantly aware of the signals others are giving.

*Crossed arms + folded arms – reluctance, defensiveness. Crossed arms display a separating or protective barrier. This can be caused by several things, including concern or severe animosity or being too tired/bored or being attentive and interested. Note that people also cross their arms when feeling cold, so be cautious not to misinterpret the signal.

*Crossed arms + clenched fists – hostile defensiveness. Generally, clenched fists are used to reinforce aggression, stubbornness, while crossed arms reinforce lack of empathy.

*Gripping one's own upper arms – insecurity. Gripping your upper arms while they're folded is basically hugging yourself, which is an attempt to reassure unsafe or unhappy feelings.

*One arm across the body clasping the other by the side (female) – nervousness. This is a protective signal used by women, and is self-hugging as well.

*Arms held behind the body with hands – authority, confidence. This is displayed by members of the royal family, police officers, teachers, armed forces officer, and so forth.

*Holding handbag in front of the body – nervousness. A protective signal as well.

*Holding papers across the chest – nervousness. This is a protective signal as well used mostly by men, especially with the arm across the chest

*Adjusting tie, watchstrap, cuff, etc. using one arm across the body – nervousness. A protective barrier as well.

*Hands/arms covering the genital region – nervousness. This is a protective barrier used by men.

*Holding a drink in front with both hands – nervousness. This is a protective signal as well.

*Holding drink on one side while seated with hand from the other side – nervousness. Another protective signal.

*Scratching or touching shoulder using one arm across the body – nervousness. A protective signal as well.

Chapter 22: Business Body Language Do's

And Don'ts

Body language is such an important factor in the world today that body language experts are highly valued in forensic careers, psychiatry, counseling, and even in human resource management, and other positions in the corporate world, as more and more entrepreneurs are realizing that incorporating appropriate gestures and body language can help their rapport with their clients and promote their brand effectively.

Reading body language and learning which poses and gestures to use can go a long way in winning someone's heart. It's also going to be better when body language can help win the boss' heart.

In business, presentation means everything. From the clothes to the posture, people in the corporate world have to always assume the proper appearance and ambience. It's not enough to be good at numbers and money, one has to be good at gauging clients' reactions and using body language to seal a deal and get on the boss' good side.

Anyone who wants to succeed in business should never underestimate the power of body language in getting a point across or selling merchandise. No matter how big or small the business is, or whether it's run by a corporation or one person, every entrepreneur has to **persuade** the client.

Do's

Always greet everyone with a smile. Even if it has been a rough day, a smile can instantly make a client or a co-worker like looking at or speaking to you.

Turn your entire body to someone you're talking to, because if only your head is facing them, they will think that you are not fully invested in the topic, which could really cause a client to throw a tantrum.

When making a presentation, move around with pauses in between. Staying still in just one place will make your presentation boring and forgettable.

Clients, colleagues, and employers will remember the more animated ones that seem to light up the room every time they speak. Also, talk to your clients, not your computer.

Use your hand gestures appropriately. Don't take copy the antics of speakers who make a speech with their hands only on the stand. Learn from orators who talk with their hands. When your palms are facing up, this means that you are willing and open for suggestion. When your palms are facing down, you are essentially telling someone to make a solid decision.

Lean slightly forward in a meeting or conversation. This signals that you are eager to start, but laid-back enough to not look **too** eager, like a teacher's pet or a sycophant. When you talk, lean forward, but lean back to indicate that you are letting someone take the stage and say their piece.

In business, it's always a must to treat your clients like you would an old friend – you're always pleased to see them.

Although you act familiar, always abide by the level of proximity or distance within the boundaries of your relationship. The average proximity would be within 1.2-2.4 meters, but if you and your client know each other well, you can stay within 46 centimeters-1.2 meters of your client.

Place your hands a foot beyond your waist on either side of your body. This open gesture is helpful when dealing with an angry co-worker. Don't match the tension in the room with threatening postures.

Aside from knowing what to do, one should also know what **not** to do:

Don'ts

Slouching is a no-no. Poor posture will give the client or your boss the impression that you either are not taking things professionally, or are not confident about something. Entrepreneurs, to sell their brand, must also sell themselves.

Don't forget to mirror others. This mirroring is not plane copying movements. This means being in sync with your teammate or your client. When they lean forward, do them the courtesy of doing the same. If you don't get into the music the group is dancing to, you will find a harder time building a rapport with them.

Don't flail your arms about. Gestures are great, if they are used appropriately. Just remember not to get too carried away and throw your hands in every direction. Look energetic, not spastic.

Don't not give feedback on a topic. Patty Wood, a body language expert, said that if you don't give feedback or a suggestion on something, you will appear as someone who doesn't care or someone who was not even paying attention.

Don't cross your legs. Crossing your legs sends a signal of low acceptance. This means that a conversation is not going as well as planned, and that you are not open to the suggestion or conversation.

Don't clench your jaw or tighten your neck. You will look hostile. If you want to strangle someone, mask these facial expressions. They are called limbic responses and, according to FBI counterintelligence agent Joe Navarro, portray a reaction to a threat. Now, unless your client is threatening your life, keep your cool and school your features into a positive one.

Never cross your arms when dealing with other people. Whether you're a CEO, the employee, or a client, crossing your arms will tell others that you do not want to be friendly with someone and that you are closed-off to other forms of negotiation. When you constantly cross your arms, people will steer clear of you and be wary of you.

Don't keep something between you and the person you're talking to. Just like the woman who keeps her purse between her and a man she's not interested in, a businessman placing something in between him and his client, colleague, or boss sends a signal that he is not actually interested in talking. Employees who are constantly looking at their computer while talking to someone send the impression that they don't care about you. This is highly important for receptionists who will be receiving potential clients.

Carol Kinsey Goman, author of several books on non-verbal communication, stated some tips in using body language for career success.

Stand tall and take up space. Confidence is such a huge factor in success. Power is greatly and nonverbally displayed through height and space. This is why posture is very important. You should keep your shoulders back, your head held high, and back straight. This will make anyone you talk to feel your confident air.

Widen your stance. When you widen your stance, you display a more open and confident vibe. This also helps relax your knees and center your weight in your lower body, which will take most of the pressure of the center of your body.

Lower your vocal pitch. Speakers should maintain an appropriate volume when speaking. Soft-spoken or loud speakers must learn to control their pitch. When you lower your voice for the clients or coworkers, however, you will be interpreted as someone who is empathetic, assured, and less frantic. You will also seem more relaxed, provided that you don't stammer or whisper unnecessarily.

Try Power Priming. Power priming is merely to remember moments that will give you confidence. This is a technique that helps you encourage and boost your self-confidence. This does not mean, however, that you should keep a log on your successes and revel in them solely. Use these experiences to recall how you sounded, looked, or acted during these moments. Smile some more and be open in your gestures.

Strike a Power Pose. The Harvard and Columbia Business Schools have conducted research on high-power poses by leaning back with the hands behind the head, feet up on a desk, or standing with the legs and arms stretched wide open. This pose increases the levels of testosterone, which is responsible for feelings of dominance and power.

Maintain positive eye contact. Anyone who wants to compete in business or succeed in their careers should learn to make proper eye contact with someone. Eye contact should not be prolonged to the point of seeming creepy, but neither should it be too short, less you look insecure or too shy.

Talk with your hands. Brain imaging has shown that a region called Broca's area is active not only when people are talking, but also when they use their hands. Gestures are linked to speech, and like the illustrators that Ekman and his partner studied, body language enhances verbal messages. People who stand rigid without moving their feet or hands will look insecure or anxious.

Use open gestures. Open gestures will show your clients or co-workers that you are approachable and open to suggestions, topics, etc. Using open gestures, with arms open wide, or palm facing upward gives a sense of transparency and honesty.

Try a steeple. Since this is a powerful gesture, a steeple will make you seem confident and authoritative. This also projects conviction and honesty.

Reduce nervous gestures. Nervous gestures will obviously make other people see the nervousness, too. You need to reduce mannerisms like fiddling with a pen, a ring, or even hair, because these will make you look insecure or unprepared. You might also come off as disinterested, unfocused, or not serious enough. Being still without movements, however, will also make you look like a robot, and will not endear you to other people.

Smile. A smile really is a powerful thing. According to research from Duke University, most people remember those who smiled at them. Using a functional magnetic resonance imaging (fMRI), the Duke University researchers found that the reward center in the brain or the orbitofrontal cortices were more active when people recalled the names of people who smiled.

Perfect your handshake. Most people will shake hands as introduction. This is also the time when most people will judge someone in just a matter of seconds. A handshake has to be firm to mean that you are serious and formal, but also warm and gentle to show an amicable attitude.

The Right Body Language in an Interview

"A candidate can give out thousands of non-verbal cues within the first minute of meeting a hiring manager, and those messages make more of an impact than the words that you use during the interview," says Patti Wood, a body language expert.

Accordingly, candidates will be judged and evaluated even before they sit for an interview. Their clothes, the way they move, their facial expressions, and their gestures will all speak volumes about them.

Wood encourages candidates to smile when the interviewer greets them. They should use a firm but warm hand for a shake. Keep the appropriate distance between you and the interviewer. "Don't freeze", he said. Most candidates will stand rigid in front of their interviewer.

Using gestures is encouraged. Gestures will tell the interviewer that you are being open and expressive. Interviewers will also look at your gestures to gauge your personality and attitude towards the company. Body language will tell the interviewer whether you are someone who can work under pressure, perform well with enthusiasm, and communicate effectively during and after the interview.

Here are body language signs you should avoid during an interview:

Weak handshake. According to Wood, "The secret to a great handshake is palm-to-palm contact. Slide your hand down into the web of theirs and make palm-to-palm contact. Lock thumbs with the hiring manager, and apply as much pressure as he or she does."

Invading personal space. Be mindful of the right distance that you should keep when facing your interviewer. Don't stand too close, and don't be too familiar with them.

Crossing your arms. Whatever reason you have for crossing your arms, you will come off as defensive, not in agreement, or uncomfortable. Crossing the arms will make your interviewer think that you are closed-off and that you are not open or willing.

Playing with your hair. Playing with your hair might turn your interviewer off. It's a stress comfort cue that will make you seem nervous, anxious, or too laid-back. While the hiring manager wants to see someone who has grace under pressure, he certainly does not want to see someone who's too comfortable like the interview isn't even a big deal.

Bad posture. "Asymmetrical body language can make you look confused or dishonest," Wood says. You have to sit straight and present a solid front. When you slouch, you will not look professional. When you lean too much into the chair, you will **still** look unprofessional.

Lack of eye contact. Making eye contact is always crucial in every conversation. Remember that you should not stare too long or too short. Look away once in a while, but always remain attentive to what the interviewer is saying.

Looking like you're not interested. Your facial expression is the first thing the interviewer will notice. Be attentive and expressive. Sometimes your anxiety will be clear on your face. School your features to make it look like you're enjoying the interview and are genuinely expressing your thoughts and ideas.

Not smiling. This can be the biggest faux pas you will commit in an interview. Even if the hiring manager is all frowns and somber looks, smile. Even if the room seems dim, brighten it up. A genuine smile will send a message that you are a person with a happy disposition and any company will be lucky to have someone like you. Also, people are almost always drawn to someone who smiles. Just remember to keep it real but subtle.

Fidgeting. Fidgeting is the most obvious sign of being nervous. When you catch yourself touching your face, rubbing your nose, playing with your tie, biting your nails or twirling a pen, **stop**. This is a very distracting movement and the interviewer will most likely get annoyed at your restlessness.

Hiding your hands. Hands with the palm and wrist visible will give the message that you are being honest and true. Patti Wood says, "Don't sit on your hands or hide them in your lap," Wood says. "Place them on the arms of your chair or the desk or use them to gesture. Gesturing makes you look more expressive, and the interviewer can read how open and honest you are by looking at your hands."

Even with these body language gestures to avoid, the most important thing you need to do in an interview is to be confident and know everything you need about the job you're applying for, and to show that you can do the job. Remember that body language can replace, emphasize, or confirm your words. Without the substance of your qualifications, though, body language is hollow and useless. Use body language as a tool, not as a crutch.

Chapter 23: The Psychology Of Body Language

In psychology body language using nonverbal communication dates back way before Sigmund Freud, B.F. Skinner, Ivan Petrovich Pavlov entered the arena. There were many others before him, Wilhelm Wundt, William James, Ulric Neisser (cognitive psychology), and many more. Yet, each of these notable scholars was no stranger to the use of nonverbal body language to communicate. Perhaps the oldest humans ever using nonverbal body language to communicate dates back to **prehistoric man** and to the **human evolution chain of Homo archaic Homo sapiens** to the **Cradle of Humankind** and beyond...

In psychology, we see some nonverbal clues, cues, or flags used to communicate in other ways.

For example, in a clinical situation, hospital, or similar setting, a person may use **blurred vision** and **blindness** to convey guilt. Perhaps a Psychiatric Attendant accused a person of stealing a comb and brush from another person on a particular ward. The person being accused may say, "I cannot see how I could have stolen it?"

Here we see a verbal confrontation shored up by a nonverbal body language technique in which the accused closes their eyes and begins to walk around the ward feeling their way around objects in their path.

Another occurrence may be the person whose **hand became paralyzed** after they had stolen extra food from the kitchen; reasoning **how could I have stolen the food when you can see my hand is paralyzed.**

We also may see someone holding their chest, signifying in a nonverbal matter using body language to communicate that they have a **load on their chest**. Others may use pain in their shoulder to signify a desire to **hit someone aggressively**. While another may contact **neurodermatitic itching** as a nonverbal way of communicating **my boss gets under my skin.**

In all uses of nonverbal body language communications, the posturing, gestures, and other types of body movements appear to take place internationally on ongoing basis; some conscious and others unconsciously.

 In other situations, a person may sleep for twenty hours because it was better to sleep 20-hours than hurt myself. **A student in a cafeteria may pick up a chair and move it closer to another group of students because he or she** wishes closeness or wishes inclusion **in the group.**

Psychologists who recognize nonverbal body language communication among those they work with and help have an upper advantage when they are able to interpret the behaviors used by those in their charge to communicate nonverbally, as illustrated by the person who may have developed a **pain in his chest**; which may be due to sadness over relatives that have not visited in a long while, or may involve problems with a spouse, a child, or loved ones.

Chapter 24: How To Spot The Personality Type?

The accurate way to evaluate the Myers Briggs personality type of people is by identifying the cognitive functions that they use in a variety of different situations. It requires a thorough knowledge of the pattern, clear insight and ample patience to evaluate the type of personality accurately. But when you take necessary steps to learn to do this, this can definitely act as a valuable tool. It will help you to understand and connect with people around you.

Once you spot the personality type, you can further dig into details on the communication strategies these people use. This will help to align your method and interact with them accordingly.

Communication strategies based on personality types

Communication style is identified by the way people appear or attempt to appear during their interaction process. These can be distinguished by paying attention to the way they usually relate to people they communicate with, how they interpret the messages, the way they react, etc. It is true that different personality types process and communicate the information in a different manner.

For instance, someone with the ENFJ personality trait will communicate easily with people who have the following personality types:

-ENFJ

-ENFP

-INFJ

-INFP

All these people belong to the NF (Intuition-Feeling) group. Similarly, the ENFJ person may not necessarily communicate well with individuals belonging to the ST (Sensing-Thinking) group – ESTJ, ESTP, ISTJ, and ISTP. What is the reason? The ST people communicate and process information in a logical way while the NF people give more importance to emotions.

When the famous psychologist Carl G Jung introduced the personality types, he characterized people by two dimensions. They represented the two opposite personality types:

-Sensing Vs. Intuition (S-N)

-Thinking Vs. Feeling (T-F)

This, in turn, formed four possible personality groups with each of them having distinctive personality characteristics. They were referred as:

-ST (Sensing-Thinking)

-NT (Intuition-Thinking)

-SF (Sensing – Feeling)

-IF (Intuition – Feeling)

How to determine the personality types?

If you want to know whether the other person is a Sensing (S) or Intuitive (N) type, then it is important to understand the characteristics that describe the said person.

Let us first look at the characteristics of the <u>Sensing (S) Vs. Intuition (N) type</u>:

Sensing (S)

-Practical and realistic

-Completely depends on numbers, facts, and specifics

-Concentrates on the current issues or problems

-Present-oriented

Intuition (N)

-Intuitive and inspirational

-Believes in theories, new development trends, and perceptions.

-Focuses on bigger things

-Future-oriented

We will now get into the characteristic details of the <u>Thinking (T) Vs. Feeling (F)</u> type:

Thinking (T)

-Regulated by reasoning and logical thinking

-Displays unbiased and neutral behavior

-More objective and cold

-Utilizes objective methodologies for problem-solving and decision-making

Feeling (F)

-Gives importance to emotions and feelings

-Sympathetic and concerning to others

-Provides support and warmth during much-needed times.

-Decision-making and problem-solving is done based on intuition and gut feeling

-Gives importance to values and ethics

What is the preferred communication style?

The four distinctive personality groups (ST, NT, SF, and NF) have their own style for communicating with other people. It is therefore important to follow the pointers mentioned below based on the personality traits while interacting with the respective person.

Remember the following when you interact with these people:

ST (Sensing - Thinking)

-Be specific with details

-Display confidence and have a proper reasoning on whatever you talk

-Talk about advantages and profits

-Provide demos and example, i.e., use visual examples during the conversation

NT (Intuition – Thinking)

-Reason out the details clearly and be specific

-Use diagrams and visual examples

-Mention theories and concepts while explaining things

-They love challenges – give them one!

-Have intellectual (cognitive) capabilities – so talk accordingly.

-Always mention the bigger picture when discussing any subject or issues

SF (Sensing – Feeling)

-Always be expressive and supportive

-Display confidence

-Talk about profits and advantages

-Cite examples and live scenarios

-Respect the emotions and feelings

NF (Intuition – Feeling)

-Have proper reasoning during the conversations

-Express yourself

-Use theories, concepts, visual examples, etc

-Respect their intuition

-Talk about the bigger picture

-Challenge them

-Get into detail on the issue or the subject discussed

How easy is it to understand people based on the personality?

There are few things that are easy to understand in people while there are a few others which are quite difficult to understand. How often have you wondered about the weird behavior displayed by your spouse? Sometimes you get so frustrated with the situation that you either quit attempting to understand the opposite sex or react aggressively.

Let us look at the things that are easy to understand in the people with the following personality traits:

ST (Sensing - Thinking)

-Rules (they abide by protocols, laws, regulations, procedures, etc.)

-Resources (this would mean money, materials, equipment, tools, etc.)

-Execution (before they execute or implement things, they look at practical solutions, reality, way things are accomplished or practiced, etc.)

-Examination (analyzing things in detail, reading between the lines, trying to understand the nuances, ensuring the proper details are collected before finalizing on the decision, etc.)

-They have a unique way of doing things.

NT (Intuition - Thinking)

-*Trendsetter*

-Different ideas and concepts

-Assess things based on the quality and value of a person or thing

-Concentrates on characteristics

-Analyzes details and finalizes on the solutions

-They give importance to expert opinions and analyst reviews

-Pays attention to paradoxical facts (these facts might challenge the already followed practices and beliefs which may, however, be the truth)

-Gives importance to the previous events and history to decide on the future.

-They work towards getting the desired outcome and focus on how events may shape.

-Believes in the consequences of actions

SF (Sensing - Feeling)

-More into emotions

-Casual chatting

-Goes by hunch and guesswork (they usually get the feeling of something is going to happen even though there is no strong reason to back the same)

-Have a specific way of doing things

-Gives importance to beliefs and gut instincts

-Try to gauge others by the way they look or appear (style, fashion, etc.)

NF (Intuition - Feeling)

-Values and ethics

-Importance to emotions and feelings

-Follows the teachings and history (pays attention to the previous events)

-Respects opinions given by analyst and goes by expert reviews

-More specific about appearance, fashion, style, etc

-Inclined towards futuristic goals

Birth order and personality

You might have often heard from older people that it is always the eldest child in the family who takes up responsibility. It is also said that children with no siblings will be more demanding and egotistic. Do you think these are just stereotypes? Or does our birth order really shape our personality?

In the late 1920s, Sigmund Freud and Alfred Adler (his colleague and friend) started the birth order theory. According to Alfred Adler, the birth order in a family affects the personality of the person.

Oldest child / First-born

The first-born in a family often tends to be dominant, displays leadership qualities and is more conservative. The reason for this behavior is that they are the ones who are mostly responsible to take care of their younger siblings. Since this gets imbibed into their character as a child, they grow up to be caring and compassionate. They like to take initiative and can become good parents.

Second child / Middle-born

The middle-born usually struggles to outshine their older sibling as the elder sister or brother will have already been the pacesetter. These kids are ambitious and are hardly ever selfish. Since they have been struggling to outshine since childhood, they often set unrealistic goals for themselves. This results in more failures, but since they know how to cope with the difficulties in life, they emerge stronger than ever.

Youngest child / Last-born

By default, it is the youngest of the lot who always gets pampered in a family. They get lot of care not only from their parents but also from their siblings. This results in them being dependent and immature when they grow up. On the other hand, these kids are highly motivated as they are compelled (by external and internal factors) to do better than their older siblings. They often achieve big successes in the field they choose. They turn out to be the most talented artists, extraordinary musicians, best athletes, etc. The last-born usually is outgoing and friendly.

The Only Child

Since the kid doesn't have any siblings to compete with, they end up racing with their father. Being the single kid and the only child in the family, they get excessively pampered by their parents. This leads to expecting the same from the others too. They love to be the center of attraction anywhere and everywhere. These kids are highly dependent and often have difficulty interacting with peers or colleagues when they grow up. However, many children who are the only kid in the family have become perfectionists and have achieved the goals they set for themselves.

Adopted child

The scenario is no different for adopted kids. In this case, the age at which the child was adopted plays a major role in exhibiting their respective personality traits. If the child was younger at the adoption stage, he or she would be completely under the care of his or her adoptive parents. As time goes by, they would take up the position in the existing family tree.

Let us try to understand this with examples – if a family who already has a four-year-old child adopts a one-year-old child (who is the first-born to his biological parents), the adopted kid will become the baby of the family (i.e., youngest) despite the fact that he is the firstborn.

But, if a family with a ten-year-old kid adopts a seven-year-old kid (who is the first-born to his biological parents), he will still act as the firstborn in his new family even though he has an elder brother.

Parenting and Birth order determines the behavior

Being the first-born in a family, the child is naturally an experiment for the new parents. They tend to follow trial and error process while raising their kid. Some parents overly pamper their kid and give them whatever they need. This naturally affects his or her behavior when they grow up. Few parents are attentive, strict and neurotic about their kid. This often results in the child becoming a perfectionist as he or she has always been striving to satisfy and make his parents happy.

When you look at a contrasting scenario where the couple decides to have a second child, their way of raising the new kid will be entirely different. Since they have already had their experiences with their first-born, they might be less attentive and stricter to the second kid. This might result in the second kid being less of a perfectionist and more of a people-pleaser. This is because he didn't get enough attention when compared to his or her elder sibling.

Though the birth order plays an important role in attributing to the personality traits, it is also the parenting that matters when it comes to shaping the child's behavior and attitude.

CPSIA information can be obtained
at www.ICGtesting.com
Printed in the USA
BVHW040906180520
579849BV00009B/373